THE PENTECOSTAL REALITY

THE PENTECOSTAL REALITY

J. Rodman Williams
Author of ERA OF THE SPIRIT

LOGOS INTERNATIONAL
Plainfield, New Jersey 07060

International Standard Book Number: 0-88270-016-2
Library of Congress Catalog Card Number: 72-91-777

Scripture quotations, unless otherwise indicated, are from the
Revised Standard Version of the Bible, copyrighted 1946 and
1952.

To

my mother

Preface

This book consists of several articles written for various occasions in the last few years. I have entitled it *The Pentecostal Reality* since this is the general theme that holds them together.

The first article, with the same title as the book, "The Pentecostal Reality," was written for the British publication, *A Voice of Faith,* Summer issue, 1971. It was also given as an address at the National Presbyterian Conference on the Holy Spirit, St. Louis, Missouri, January 11-14, 1972.

"The Event of the Holy Spirit" was written for the Institute of Ecumenical and Cultural Research, Collegeville, Minnesota, and read at an Institute seminar on October 6, 1971.

The article, "A New Era in History," was prepared for the International Conference on the Fellowship of the Holy Spirit, University of Surrey, England, July 12-17, 1971, and given in part as an address during that conference.

"Pentecostal Spirituality" was written for the first international Roman Catholic-Pentecostal/charismatic dialogue held in Zürich, Switzerland, June 19-24, 1972.

The paper, "The Holy Spirit and Evangelism," was written for the Task Force on Evangelism, Presbyterian Church in the United States, Summer, 1966.

"The Holy Trinity" is a sermon first preached at the University Presbyterian Church, Austin, Texas, on June 7, 1970.

Since these articles were written variously for magazine, seminar, international conference, ecumenical dialogue, task force, and pulpit presentation, there are differences in approach, style, and length. Also because the articles were written independently of one another, there may be some overlapping. My hope is that the diversity of occasions and audiences for which they were done will make for freshness and interest throughout.

It is my prayer that the Lord will use these pages for the praise of His glory.

CONTENTS

1

The Pentecostal Reality

In the "worldwide Pentecost" now occurring I should like to set forth some of my reflections under the heading of "The Pentecostal Reality." I do this with more than a little excitement because of my conviction that this is a movement of the Holy Spirit which has great significance for the whole of Christendom. For the sake of clarity and conciseness I shall summarize my thoughts in five basic statements.

1. *The most important happening in the church today is the rediscovery of the Pentecostal reality.*

There is much transpiring in the life and activity of the church that can lay claim to being of critical importance. One has only to recall the variety of things happening in such areas as confessional restatement, liturgical reform, improvement in evangelistic methods, search for new forms of ministry, concern for more relevant social involvement, and multiple ecumenical activity. The church today is obviously in much ferment and seeking almost desperately to discover some secret, some strategy whereby it can find its way in a very difficult time. In the midst of all of this a strange thing — exciting to many, baffling to

1

others — is also occurring which seemingly has little relation to these various things, namely, the rediscovery of the Pentecostal reality.

This rediscovery is of such foundational importance that the whole church needs seriously and openly to consider it. By no means is there any intention of discounting the significance of the church's varied efforts in faith and life — for God is surely at work in many ways. But beyond these something is happening in the lives of many people of so vital a nature as to make possible new impulses of power for the complete round of Christian activity. Nothing therefore in the life of the church today calls for more urgent consideration than this contemporary rediscovery of the Pentecostal reality.

2. By "the Pentecostal reality" is meant the coming of God's Holy Spirit in power to the believing individual and community.

Among countless numbers of people today in many churches an event or experience is happening which makes vivid the narrative of Acts 1 and 2 as contemporary event. What they may have considered before as more or less interesting history of the first days of the church — and some of it rather strange (especially Acts 2:1-4)—has suddenly become personally real. For they too have experienced a coming of the Holy Spirit wherein God's presence and power has pervaded their lives. It may not have been quite like "wind" and "fire," but they do confess, in joy and humility, that they know what it means to be "filled with the Holy Spirit." There has been a breakthrough of God's Spirit into their total existence — body, soul, and spirit — reaching into the conscious and subconscious depths, and setting loose powers hitherto unknown. Through the operation of the Holy Spirit many have found themselves (like those on the Day of Pentecost) speaking in "other tongues" and declaring the mighty works of God in ways transcending all human ability. Power is there — and this includes a heightened capacity to witness to others about the grace of God in Jesus Christ. By the Holy Spirit there is fresh courage and boldness, and however faulty the human words, they carry conviction because they come freighted with the power of the Holy Spirit. The minds and hearts of those who hear are intensely probed by the Spirit, and many find new life and salvation. But this is not the whole story, because the powers set loose are not only those energizing witness (whereby God is extraordinarily praised and men are deeply moved), but also those whereby "wonders and signs" are now performed (cf. Acts 2:43). Multiple acts of healing and deliverance, previously unimagined, now become a part of ongoing Christian life.

This, as described, is something of "the Pentecostal reality." There is nothing here totally foreign to what Christians have always known and experienced; however, this reality signifies a breaking in of the Holy Spirit with such effect as to point to a further dimension of His operation. Thus there is both familiarity and strangeness to the church at large — as it stands today in the midst of the Pentecostal reality.

A word needs to be added about the background of those for whom the Pentecostal reality has become personal experience. They all came into this through believing in Jesus Christ. Many had been devoted servants of Christ long before it occurred, others only a short time, some found it happening at the moment of their coming to faith. All however had experienced His forgiveness and received His grace. But at whatever time the Pentecostal reality occurred, they knew that it came from Jesus Christ; it was He through whom the Spirit was poured out (cf. Acts 2:33).

3. *The "rediscovery" refers to the fact that for the church as a whole this experience of the Pentecostal reality represents the coming to light of a dimension of the Holy Spirit's activity that has long been unrealized or overlooked.*

The word "rediscovery" is quite appropriate because what is happening today is an opening up of truth long neglected. For many it is so new, even startling, that it is hard to believe that the Pentecostal reality is a possibility within Christian faith. On the other hand, when the discovery is made, and a person enters into it, he may wonder how it could have been missed for so long! However, if he turns joyfully to his church to testify to what has happened, quite often there is antagonism and opposition — as if the Pentecostal reality were a foreign foe. Thus frequently is repeated, though at a different point, the situation of Martin Luther. His experience of "free grace" was likewise strange to many in the church of his day, and as a result Luther found himself, while praising God for this momentous rediscovery, being ostracized by his own people. *Truth, re-opened and re-lived, does not set well with tradition long established.*

What, we may ask, happened in the long tradition of the church to the knowledge and experience of the Pentecostal reality? Two things at least should be noted. First, in the Catholic tradition there has been the tendency to "sacramentalize" this reality and experience. Beyond the sacrament of baptism (wherein, according to Catholic teaching, regeneration occurs and Christian life begins) there is the sacrament of confirmation in which there is the laying on of hands

4

for the strengthening of the believer in the service of Christ. The scriptural basis often adduced is that of Acts 8:4-17, which makes a clear differentiation between baptism and the later reception of the Holy Spirit through the laying on of hands. In this confirmation the Holy Spirit is said to be given as He was to the apostles at Pentecost, and the result is that an "indelible character" is printed upon the recipient whereby his strengthening occurs. But — and here a critical question must be raised — what are the evidences that the Pentecostal reality has actually been experienced? Whatever may have been symbolized (or even objectively mediated) by the sacrament, does the confirmand ordinarily exhibit the signs of a genuine Pentecostal occurrence? The answer unfortunately must be no. Thus one can only conclude that the "sacramentalizing" of this reality has had the effect of formalizing it and thereby failing to make actual the inward experience.

Second, in the tradition of many Protestant churches, there is little or no emphasis placed on confirmation; accordingly, it is understood that the Pentecostal reality (insofar as it is considered) is included in baptism and/or regeneration. Variously it is suggested that since baptism is also "in the name of the Holy Spirit," this includes the Pentecostal "outpouring," or — particularly where "believer's baptism" is the pattern — that conversion, rebirth, regeneration, etc., is identical with the Pentecostal experience. The former understanding suffers the same problem as above mentioned, namely, the lack of personal experience. Even if there is something given in baptism, what about the inward appropriation? The latter interpretation, which identifies conversion with the Pentecostal reality, is quite difficult to maintain. By what stretch of the imagination can one see in the original Pentecostal event of Acts 2:1-4 an experience of conversion or regeneration? Also Acts 8:4-17 has to be disregarded or misinterpreted (here the Catholic tradition, despite its sacramentalism, is closer to Scripture than much Protestantism). Thus the Pentecostal reality eludes both traditional Catholicism and Protestantism through either a sacramentalism which formalizes the experience or an emphasis on baptism/regeneration that overlooks it!

It is scarcely an exaggeration, therefore, to say that this rediscovery of the Pentecostal reality in our day is of vast importance. For it is not some theological or biblical matter of relatively minor significance, but concerns the *whole dimension of power* which is available for Christian life and witness. To be sure, there is no genuine belief in Jesus Christ that is possible without the Holy Spirit (since it is He who makes faith in Christ effectual), and no consequent discipleship which is without the Holy Spirit's leading and instruction (cf. Acts 1:2). Thus the Holy Spirit is at work in all Christian faith and practice. But this must not be identified with the Pentecostal reality which is none other than the coming of the Holy Spirit to anoint the people of God with power for extraordinary praise, speech that breaks open the hardest of hearts, the performing of signs and wonders, and a boldness of witness and action that can transform the world.

4. *The word "happening" suggests that the Pentecostal reality is event, occurrence, action, and takes place in the context of God's free promise and man's open readiness.*

The "promise of the Father" (Acts 1:4) which is the "promise of the Holy Spirit" (Acts 2:33) is the assurance that stands behind the Pentecostal event. It is

6

a promise not only to the original disciples but also to those after them who believe: "For the promise is to you and your children and to all that are far off, every one whom the Lord our God calls to him" (Acts 2:39). Thus the Pentecostal reality is no chance occurrence, limited in scope, but is the fulfillment of the unfailing promise of God the heavenly Father. Accordingly, those whom God calls to Him in every generation are without exception assured that the Pentecostal reality is available to them. Those in our day for whom Pentecost has become a living experience have not hesitated to take God at His word and believe in His promise.

Because the promise is free, the Holy Spirit comes as a gift. The Pentecostal reality, therefore, is none other than "the gift of the Holy Spirit" (Acts 2:38; cf. 11:17). As a gift it cannot be earned but comes as a gracious bestowal from God the Father to His sons through Jesus Christ. Those who receive this blessing can never claim to have gained it by work or merit. One who has experienced the Pentecostal reality, therefore, can only be gladly and humbly thankful for God's gracious action.

The other side of the picture is that of openness and readiness for the promised gift. The promise is assured those who wait upon the Lord (Acts 1:4); it happens to those who devote themselves to prayer (Acts 1:14); the Spirit is given those who obey the Father (Acts 5:32). Though the gift may not be earned, it may be asked for. Indeed, the very asking (even seeking and knocking) represents the kind of readiness which is the human context for the heavenly gift — so "will the heavenly Father give the Holy Spirit to those who ask him" (Luke 11:13).

What many have found to be quite important is the need for total yieldedness to God's possession.

When from the human side there is surrender of the complete self (including, perhaps climactically, the tongue!), a willingness to let go everything for the sake of the Gospel — including reputation and security — and an emptiness of self before the Lord, He may then move in to fill the person with His power and presence.

But the sovereign God remains the free disposer of His gift of the Holy Spirit. He has promised it, so we need not doubt its coming; and if we ask, He will surely answer. But there is no guarantee as to exactly when it will take place, nor under precisely what circumstances. It happened suddenly at the Jerusalem Pentecost (Acts 2:2), surprisingly at the Gentile Pentecost (Acts 10:44), and, in our day, the element of suddenness and surprise has by no means ceased! There is simply no point at which — regardless of the number of prayers offered, the quality of yieldedness, or whatever else may be done — we can be sure of the Spirit's coming. God remains the sovereign Lord.

5. *The fact that the Pentecostal reality is being rediscovered in "the church today" could bring about a renewal of incalculable proportions.*

It is imperative that the church of today be fully acquainted with the nature of the Pentecostal reality and adopt a positive attitude toward its occurrence. Reference has been made to the opposition that often has developed against it. Doubtless, fault lies partly among those of Pentecostal experience who in many cases have misguidedly represented its significance (e.g., as a kind of superior Christianity — or even "the real thing") and thereby brought about disharmony and division. But this is only a small part of the total picture, for often, regardless of the adequacy of the witness, antipathy has been aroused. This is quite understandable in light of the fact that the tradition of the church (as noted) and, even more, the long-inherited structure of Christian faith and practice has had no adequate place for the Pentecostal experience. The Pentecostal reality thus appears as a threat; and for the sake of protecting what is already established, strong efforts are often made to repel an apparently foreign body. But now it is fervently to be hoped that, with more adequate understanding of what the Pentecostal reality means, and its signal importance for the full life of the church, a new, positive, and expectant attitude can develop.

Even more, however, than just developing a positive attitude, the church at large needs to open itself to the Pentecostal reality. There is a growing recognition among many people in the church today — clergymen and laity alike — that at the heart of much of our life and activity a deep spiritual crisis exists. Despite multiple attempts by the church at reassessment and relevance, there remains the haunting sense of something lacking or unfulfilled and a feeling of spiritual impotence. How tragic indeed when the church was intended to be a dynamic fellowship of the Spirit through whom the world is transformed! Thus, nothing is so urgent for the church throughout the world as to heed the word of the Lord: "Stay . . . until you are clothed with power from on high" (Luke 24:49). Who can begin to imagine the full scope of what might happen if the church took that command seriously?

2

The Event of the Holy Spirit

There are millions of people today who lay claim to "Pentecostal experience." They belong not only to churches called Pentecostal, but also are found in many of the traditional churches of Protestantism and in Roman Catholicism. A movement that began in the early twentieth century has now become worldwide, and thus a matter of high ecumenical significance. Herein I shall attempt to describe the focal point of Pentecostal witness, namely, the event of the Holy Spirit, and its relationship to the thought and life of the larger church.

Much may be said about the Pentecostal witness in such terms as fullness of prayer and praise, multiplication of charismatic activity, and bold witness to the Gospel, but behind all of these is testimony to an event. There was a time before; then occurred a certain event; afterward the world of the Spirit opened up. It is this special event, the event of the Holy Spirit, that now calls for careful consideration.

The expression most frequently used for this event or happening is "baptism with [or 'in'] the Holy Spirit." This refers to something that has occurred in one's own life and experience, and is the door into the new fullness of life in the Spirit.

The word "baptism" is quite expressive because of its connotation of totality. To be baptized can signify an experience of being inundated by, submerged in, or pervaded with some reality. This is well illustrated in water baptism where modes of practice vary from a pouring or sprinkling to immersion, each in its own way conveying a picture of totality. "Baptism with the Spirit" points to a whelming of the person — an event wherein man in his conscious and subconscious existence is penetrated by the Spirit of God. No level of human existence is unaffected by this divine activity.

This "baptism with the Holy Spirit," however, is not a happening in which the person is so possessed by God that he loses his own identity. Nor is the Spirit's movement an invasion wherein the self becomes subjugated and coerced into a divine pattern of activity, so that the sole actor thereafter is God. Much less is it a pantheistic absorption into deity, or a sudden transportation out of this world into another realm. "Baptism" is not subjugation, or absorption, or translation, but the actualization of a dynamic whereby the whole person is energized to fulfill new possibilities. This fulfillment does have aspects previously unknown and unrealized (for example, the "*charismata*," or "gifts of the Spirit"), since the divine Spirit is moving powerfully through the free human spirit. But at no point is there the setting aside of human activity. Indeed, quite the opposite, for it is only as the Spirit of God blows upon the human spirit that there is the release of man for fuller freedom and responsibility.

Again, this "baptism with the Holy Spirit" is not a kind of "instant sanctification." If the Spirit of God really possesses human existence, one might wonder if this does not imply that man is thereby made perfectly holy. If such were the implication, many questions would be in order: Do we see actual evidences of this holiness among those who claim such an experience; Is there any biblical basis to support a view of immediate sanctification; Does not the whole idea overlook the empirical fact of all men's continuing sinfulness? Thus it is important to recognize that "baptism with the Spirit" as such has nothing to do with holiness of character, but with penetration of life. The effect is not a certain quality of existence but a way of life in which one is open to the Spirit's activity. Therefore rather than sudden holiness, the actual situation is that as the Spirit of God lays complete claim upon a person, he begins to see not his holiness but the depths of his sinful condition. The event of the Spirit does give power for more adequate dealing with human perversity; consequently, there should be progress in sanctification. But the "baptism with the Spirit" is not in itself the accomplishment of that end.

Another expression, in addition to "baptism with the Holy Spirit," frequently used, is "filled with the Holy Spirit." This may refer likewise to the event of entrance into Pentecostal life and experience. The word "filled" — or "full" — has the advantage of expressing totality even more markedly than the word "baptism." When a person, for example, is said to be "filled with joy," everyone understands this as referring to the whole self. Such a one is rejoicing with all of his being — body, mind, spirit. Even so, to be "filled with the Spirit" is to express the situation in which the whole of human existence is activated by the divine reality.

The word "filled" also expresses with particular force the background for the operation of spiritual gifts. Because one is "filled with the Spirit," charismatic manifestations may occur. They are obvious signs and indications of Spirit-filled existence. The supernatural becomes, so to speak, natural and normal in the context of a life open to the Spirit's activity.

Other terms used for the event of the Spirit include such words as "effusion," "outpouring," even the "falling" of the Holy Spirit. Or this event may be referred to as simply the "coming" of the Spirit. The impression given by this variety of terms, in addition to totality, is forcefulness. The Spirit comes from without and with mighty impact. The event of the Spirit is no gradual, passive thing, but a decisive endowment of power and energy. When the Spirit is "poured out" or "falls," life can never be quite the same again.

Whatever the expression — "baptism," "filling," "outpouring" or otherwise — reference is thereby made to a dynamic movement of the Holy Spirit which results in a new sense of God's presence and power, various charismata becoming manifest, and the emergence of a different style of life. These things are possible only through the event of the Spirit.[1]

What now are some of the aspects of the situation in which this event of the Holy Spirit happens? First, everything centers in Jesus Christ: He is the one who "baptizes with the Holy Spirit." There is no Spirit baptism without the direct activity of Jesus Christ. It is Christ the Crucified, Risen, and Exalted Lord who pours forth the Holy Spirit. However much one may rightly stress the activity of the Holy Spirit, this is not a "pneumacentric" but a "Christocentric" event. It is not the Spirit who does the baptizing, but Christ Him-

---

1. Fr. Kilian McDonnell writes that "the issue in Pentecostalism is not tongues, but fullness of life in the Holy Spirit, openness to the power of the Spirit, and the exercise of all the gifts of the Spirit." *Catholic Pentecostalism: Problems in Evaluation,"* p. 9.

self. Accordingly, this understanding of the event of the Spirit is quite different from any so-called Spirit movement that tends to disregard the work of the historic Christ, or that seeks for spiritual reality in a direct, unmediated relationship with God. God the Father is the ultimate source, but it is through Jesus Christ the Lord that the Holy Spirit is given.

Second, "Pentecost," while referring to a past event (narrated in Acts 2), is likewise a present experience. The event was, and is, two-sided: Christ the Lord on the one hand, and those who are "baptized" on the other. Hence, Pentecost represents more than a once-for-all incident in the life of the early church. The Spirit was not poured out upon the community of faith on that first day to remain therein until the end of time. Such a view fails to understand Pentecost as both past and present, and leaves little room or expectation for the reality to occur among people now. If the event is to take place today, there must be the recognition of its continuing possibility.

Third, this event occurs within the arena of faith. Faith in Jesus Christ as Savior and Lord is the essential precondition; only those who so believe may share in the Pentecostal reality. However, the event itself is not always coincidental with the inception of faith; it may occur then or at a later time. In fact many would testify to "baptism with the Spirit" as happening somewhere along the way of faith, not at the beginning. Others would attest that this experience occurred at the first moment of faith. But the usual witness is the former, namely, that there had been belief for some time before the Pentecostal event took place. In either case faith remains the context for the outpouring of the Holy Spirit.

Fourth, the event of the Spirit cannot be simply patterned or programmed. The original Pentecost came about suddenly, and there remains an element of surprise in its occurrence. God the Holy Spirit acts in sovereign unpredictability and His ways cannot be computerized. On the human side there is also a wide range of spiritual susceptibility, so that not everyone is ready at the same time for the operations of God to occur. There may be an unwillingness to surrender oneself to the Spirit, an unreadiness to let the barriers drop, a holding in reserve certain areas of the personality. But when something inside finally gives way, the Pentecostal event may happen. Prayer, earnest and continuing, is often the background for the occurrence of "baptism with the Spirit." Commonly the matrix for the event of the Spirit is an attitude of openness and expectancy, of acknowledged spiritual hunger and thirst. None of this, however, is a way of achieving or earning the Spirit, for the Holy Spirit comes as an act of God's grace. The element of spontaneity, unpredictability, surprise remains throughout; for it is with God's gracious and free Spirit that man has to do.

Fifth, the event of the Spirit is basically a community happening. It often comes about when people are gathered for worship and fellowship; especially at a time of praise there may be the breakthrough of a new dimension of God's activity and power. Those present may not be seeking this "baptism," as such, nor others directly ministering to them; but the atmosphere may become so filled with the Spirit of God that miraculous things occur. Manifestations of the gifts of the Spirit (cf. I Cor. 12-14) may become the occasion for the event of the Spirit. At such a gathering there is often the personal ministry of the community, either through a few persons or an individual, for those who admit their need. Sometimes this ministry is accompanied by the laying on of hands for the coming of the Holy Spirit. Whether the moving of the Spirit happens when one is in the company of others or alone, there remains the sense of the community participating in the event.

A concluding word: In the event of the Holy Spirit there is both a giving and a receiving. The expression, "the gift of the Holy Spirit," may be used to speak of the divine side of the event; the "receiving of the Holy Spirit," to express the human side of accepting the gift. The event of the Spirit is altogether God's gracious doing; man earns nothing, adds nothing, he merely receives. Consequently, there are no conditions or requirements to be met, no stairs to climb or hoops to jump through, but simply the reception of a freely offered gift. Still, without receiving, the gift remains afar. "Baptism with the Holy Spirit" is an occasion of both giving and receiving; and it has been so since the first Pentecost.

Now it is time to focus on the radicalism of the Pentecostal witness. By "radicalism" is first meant the root (*"radix"*) of a certain reality that has come to be experienced. The person of Pentecostal experience does not begin with a theology about the Holy Spirit, not even a biblical teaching as such, but with something that has happened in his life. He doubtless has heard about the Holy Spirit, possibly even theologized thereabout, and he may have had some or much biblical acquaintance — and all of this will surely feed into his experience — but the Pentecostal is essentially talking about something that is deeply existential.[2] Hence the expressions used thus far — "baptism," "filling," "gift," "reception," and others — though

---

2. Larry Christenson writes in his *Speaking in Tongues,* "There is a sound theology for the baptism with the Holy Spirit. But the baptism with the Holy Spirit is not a theology to be discussed and analyzed. It is an experience one enters into" (p. 40).

biblical, are not primarily understood by exegeting certain texts. Rather, these terms are helpful ways of defining what has occurred. Others may wonder why the Pentecostal witness makes so much use of this kind of language (for example, the psychologist who may look for more human explanations than "Holy Spirit baptism" or the biblical scholar who may question if certain scriptural terminology is being used properly). Nonetheless, the person of Pentecostal experience finds in such language the biblical way of expressing what has taken place in his life. Until some better way comes along of saying what has happened, he will doubtless continue to talk about "baptism with the Holy Spirit," and the like. What else conveys with such force a reality that has gripped his existence?

But "radicalism" also means something drastic, a position or view that is not held in the same way by others, and thus considered to be extreme. In this sense there is something radical about the Pentecostal position, if for no other reason than that most people talk little about such matters as "the event of the Spirit" and "baptism with the Spirit." They will speak, for example, of the Spirit's work in inspiring Scripture, in convicting of sin, in enabling faith in Jesus Christ, and in sanctification; but generally they do not recognize this event of the Spirit except as an incident that happened at Pentecost long ago. Many presume to know at least about baptism, but usually this is baptism in water with almost no thought about "baptism with the Spirit." Who talks, they may inquire, about "baptism in the Spirit" except Pentecostals? Thus there seems to be something radical sounding, possibly sectarian, in the Pentecostal testimony.

From the perspective of much traditional Christianity there is a strangeness about the whole area of the Holy Spirit. Talk about the Holy Spirit is not common, especially in Western Christendom. Neither Protestants nor Roman Catholics generally feel comfortable when they encounter the frequent use of Holy Spirit language in Pentecostal witness; the first reaction is often one of defensiveness and perhaps a repetition of traditional views. The strangeness, however, may not be the fault of the Pentecostal, but of a deficiency and neglect on the part of the church at large.[3]

Christendom has actually never dealt adequately with the doctrine of the Holy Spirit. Trinitarian and Christological issues were at the forefront in the days of the early ecumenical councils, but the pneumatological question was always incidental. The Reformation, with its focus on the issue of salvation, particularly justification, by no means satisfactorily treated pneumatology. On the left of Roman Catholicism and classical Protestantism, spiritualist and enthusiastic movements have at times arisen as an attempted corrective, but these have tended to slip away from a Christological center. As a result Christendom has suffered from lack of an adequate pneumatology that does not sacrifice the great gains in Trinitarian, Christological, and soteriological understanding. There has been a tendency to subsume the person and work of the Holy Spirit under that of Christ with the result that the church has been able to find little place for

---

3. The Faith and Order Commission of the World Council of Churches at its meeting in August, 1971 (see *Faith and Order: Louvain 1971*), approved a document on "Spirit, Order and Organization" that includes the following pertinent statements: "The emergence and growth of Independent Churches in Africa, of Pentecostal Churches and of Pentecostalism within the established Churches could point to some deficiency of traditional Roman Catholicism and Protestantism. Theology and practice of these Churches has to a large extent neglected the Holy Spirit, except for some standard affirmations about his continuing presence.... The doctrine of the Holy Spirit and even more the sensitivity to his active presence in the Church and the world were and still are underdeveloped in the western tradition of Christianity" (pp. 117, 131-132). Also an excerpt from the document adopted on "Baptism, Confirmation and Eucharist" may be noted: "The development of Pentecostal movements reminds the historic Churches how much they have neglected life in the Spirit" (p. 41).

the special operation of the Holy Spirit.[4] The Holy Spirit has been recognized as fully God, third person in the Trinity, but His particular field of activity has not stood out with sufficient clarity.

Most of Western Christendom, furthermore, speaks seldom of the Holy Spirit's coming to the life of man. There is a mystical tradition, more in Catholicism than in Protestantism, but it tends to stress the elevation of man to God rather than the descent of God in the Spirit to man. Also there is generally strong resistance to any idea of ordinary human beings participating in the activity of God. Here the Eastern Church, with its sense of divine immanence and view of the Incarnation as making man partaker of the divine nature, may be more congenial than the Western tradition with the Pentecostal stress on the coming and activity of the Spirit.

The usual Protestant objection to the Pentecostal witness is that it does not represent an improvement or corrective in the area of the Holy Spirit but a distortion — a shifting away from a soteriological ("salvation history") to a pneumatic orientation. This stress on the Holy Spirit and His activity is viewed as detracting from the centrality of Christ and His saving work. Such emphasis seems to provide a different focus — not salvation but "baptism with the Holy Spirit" — thereby subverting both Bible and Christian faith.

Thus Protestant reading of the New Testament rarely makes room for a special event of the Holy Spirit. Moreover there is largely silence in the confessions of the churches, and among the theologians this subject is seldom treated. If an interpretation of such an expression as "baptism with the Holy Spirit" is at-

---

4. This will be discussed with fuller detail in chapter III, "A New Era in History." Also see my book, *The Era of the Spirit*, p. 53, text and footnote, for brief delineation.

tempted, it is usually identified with God's work of regeneration. It is often viewed as the inner side of baptism with water, namely, that even as water symbolizes outer cleansing, "baptism with the Spirit" refers to inward purification. Thus the event of the Spirit becomes the cleansing of the old, the birth of the new, the marvel of regeneration. Hence this activity of the Spirit is understood as making efficacious the redemptive work of Christ by applying it to the individual; it is the subjective side of salvation. Accordingly, "baptism with the Spirit" is viewed as the beginning of Christian initiation. It is assumed that the event of the Spirit is nothing other than the coming to birth of the new man in Christ. There is little recognition of "baptism with the Spirit" as referring to a further action of God which is the particular work of the Holy Spirit.

To reply: One may express agreement about the role of the Holy Spirit in the origination of Christian life and about the activity of the Holy Spirit in sanctification, but this is not the whole picture. First, as earlier noted, something has happened in the lives of many people for which the Protestant explanation is not satisfactory. They have known an experience of the Spirit's power and presence that cannot be identified with initiation of new life in Christ but only with a movement of the Holy Spirit whereby a further dimension opens up. Neither can this experience be compared with sanctification, the life of growth in holiness, since it rather has the character of empowering event. Second, this Pentecostal understanding of a special event of the Spirit is actually more in line with the essential biblical witness than is traditional Protestant interpretation. The general Protestant viewpoint does justice neither to personal experience nor to all the data in Scripture.

Since this latter point is crucial for Protestants

with a long emphasis on *"sola Scriptura,"* it is important to set forth some biblical justification. First of all, there was an event of the Spirit, according to Acts 2:1-4, which was neither related to the beginning of Christian faith nor to some aspect of sanctification. Those "baptized with the Holy Spirit," or "filled with the Holy Spirit," on the day of Pentecost were already believers, and what happened to them was not a "making holy." Rather here was a new dimension of the Spirit's activity in relation to persons within the community of faith. The important thing was the new dimension — not some result such as regeneration or sanctification — the dimension of spiritual fullness. Out of this fullness came an overflow of praise in tongues (2:4-13), of witness to the Gospel (2:14-36), the salvation of thousands (2:37-41), and the life of the first Christian community (2:42-47). The Pentecostal reality was therefore none of these latter things, wonderful as they were, but the "baptizing," the "filling," the empowering of those who believed in order that these results might abundantly follow. If that is what the event of Spirit baptism meant for Jesus' disciples on the day of Pentecost, why should we view it otherwise in our day?

Second, despite linguistic and situational differences, several further accounts in Acts provide evidence of an event of the Spirit not identified with the initiation of faith and salvation. The narrative in Acts 8 tells of a group of people, Samaritans, who came to faith in Jesus Christ and were baptized in His name (8:4-13); however, it was not until some days later, following the laying on of hands by Peter and John, that the Holy Spirit fell upon these new believers (8:14-17). Acts 9, the first account of Paul's conversion, depicts an original crisis moment when there was recognition of Jesus as Lord (9:1-8), but it was three days before Ananias laid hands on Saul of Tarsus, and he was

22

"filled with the Holy Spirit" (9:9-19). According to Acts 19, Paul asked the question of some dozen Ephesians, "Did you receive the Holy Spirit when you believed?" (19:2), implying that faith or belief is not necessarily accompanied by the reception of the Holy Spirit. Shortly thereafter, upon their profession of faith in Christ and baptism in His name, and as a separate act, Paul laid hands upon the Ephesians for them to receive the Holy Spirit (19:3-6). Though none of these are "Pentecostal" occurrences in the sense of happening on the Day of Pentecost, the pattern is essentially the same: the gift of the Holy Spirit subsequent to the initiation of faith, thus something happening to believers. The purpose would seem identical to that of the original Pentecostal event: that the Samaritans, Paul, and the Ephesians might be empowered for the sake of the Gospel. So in the record of Acts there is a continuation of the first Pentecost — and, it might be added, further basis for what has happened in the lives of many today.[5]

Finally, to the Protestant objection of another focus beyond Christ, and thus a subverting of Scripture and faith, the Pentecostal answer has become clear. There is no leaving Christ behind for a different centering in the Holy Spirit, for it is precisely through Christ that the event of the Spirit occurs. The real problem is not one of additional focus but that the typical Protestant has difficulty recognizing the "baptizing" work of Christ with the Holy Spirit, and there-

---

5. No attempt is made above to go beyond the record in Acts. However, Acts is the only description in the New Testament of the origination of Christian communities and of the complexities and variations of the relationship between faith in Christ and the coming of the Spirit. The Epistles are written to established situations in which these things have already occurred. One may find, for example, in Ephesians 1:3-14 reference to a pattern of events not unlike Acts, but they have *already* happened. Hence, the primary use of Acts is necessary for perception into the dynamics of these interrelationships.

by comes close to eliminating from Bible and experience a vital dimension of God's activity.[6]

The traditional Roman Catholic orientation on the activity of the Holy Spirit makes for a different set of problems than those of the Protestant. One difficulty is that Catholic thought has tended to identify the original Pentecostal event with a permanent gift of the Holy Spirit to the church wherein the Holy Spirit becomes "the soul" of the church. Thus there is no need or possibility of such an event as Pentecost occurring among people thereafter. A second difficulty is that the Catholic tradition on the whole minimizes the importance of decisive moments in faith, for example, the experience of conversion. Catholicism is development — rather than crisis-oriented; hence, the sense of a before and after, as in the "baptism with the Spirit," is largely lacking. A third difficulty is the strong emphasis on sacramental grace, namely, that the Holy Spirit is objectively mediated through such sacraments as baptism and confirmation. This would seem to bind any unique gift of the Holy Spirit to the sacramental actions of the Church.

---

6. The water baptismal formula used generally by Protestants (and of course Christendom at large) is baptism "in the name of the Father and of the Son and of the Holy Spirit" (according to Matt. 28:19). Here there is recognition of a baptism also in connection with the Holy Spirit and a practice that goes beyond baptism in the name of Christ only (as in the Book of Acts). This is not unimportant, because the baptismal act points to more than a liturgical formula; it signifies introduction into ("into" may be preferable to "in" for the Greek word "*eis*") a living relationship with Father, Son, and Holy Spirit. Thus it could properly be held that everyone baptized in the Triune name has some experience of baptism "in" or "with" the Holy Spirit; consequently, what has been said thus far about "baptism with the Spirit" is not altogether foreign to the life of any regularly baptized person. For there is a sense in which the whole Pentecostal reality, or event of the Spirit, is *anticipated* in the third part of the baptismal formula. From this perspective "baptism with the Spirit" could be understood not as the wholly new but as the appropriation of what was given in baptism. This, however, by no means lessens the importance of an "event of the Spirit" whereby the potential is actualized or the anticipated brought to fulfillment. (The same could be said about baptism in the name of Father and Son; however, this is not the place to go into other aspects of the baptismal reality.) Whether one follows the line of "baptism See chapter 6, "The Holy Trinity," for further elaboration.

24

Thus here there is a limitation which does not allow for the free and unpredictable move of the Holy Spirit.

Despite these difficulties the Roman Catholic tradition is compatible with the Pentecostal viewpoint in at least three ways. First, the Catholic Church has always held in high regard the supernatural, and therefore is by no means averse to the idea of a miraculous intervention by God in human life. Second, there has been a continued emphasis in the Catholic tradition on the life of spirituality and the possibility of higher or deeper levels of faith and experience. Third, throughout Catholic history there has been sensitivity to a special implementing work of the Holy Spirit through the laying on of hands, a rite that in the fifth century came to be known as confirmation. However differently understood through the centuries, this rite has continued to bear witness to a special gift of the Holy Spirit within the life of faith.

This latter point is important for the Catholic orientation to the Pentecostal witness. For the Pentecostal there are two distinct moments: conversion and baptism with the Spirit. They may be separated from each other by years, although both belong to the full life of the Christian. The Catholic picture traditionally has been much the same, in that beyond regeneration is the further step of confirmation wherein the Holy Spirit is given for strengthening the believer in his dedication to Christ. Thus similar are the Catholic and Pentecostal perspectives, and quite different from the Protestant position that minimizes an event of the Spirit beyond the effecting of faith in Christ.

However, there are differences within this common area. One may refer first to the matter of personal experience. What the Catholic Church affirms to be given in these sacraments, the Pentecostal claims to have experienced. In baptism, according to

Catholicism, regeneration is mediated, *ex opere operato,* by the Church: all receive new birth in water by virtue of the ritual act. The same is true of confirmation: through the laying on of hands by the bishop an "indelible character" is made regardless of personal response. The essential thing is the sacramental action. In contrast, for the Pentecostal, what is decisive is not the action of the church but the experience.[7] Another difference concerns the matter of ministry. The Pentecostal does not view as essential either the ministry of an ordained clergyman or the laying on of hands. In personal ministry, laymen, equally with clergymen, may serve — and sometimes this is done not by one person but by a group. Nevertheless, either type of ministry is dispensable, since God through Jesus Christ may pour out His Spirit without human mediation. Thus the laying on of hands, while often used by the Spirit, is by no means necessary. God moves as He wills in His freedom.

In conclusion: The Pentecostal witness represents a fresh way of thought and practice within the prevailing patterns of Western Christendom. It clearly poses the question of how to relate this witness to traditional Protestantism and Roman Catholicism. However, the prior question for the whole church, I would urge, is this: Is it possible that the Pentecostal is witnessing to something that is needed by all? It could be that the fresh experience of the Pentecostal reality by the church at large would signalize a new era of the presence and power of the Holy Spirit.

---

7. For some Catholic Pentecostals there is a serious attempt to bring together a unity of sacramental action and inward experience by speaking of "baptism with the Spirit" as "experiencing the effect of confirmation." See *Confirmation and the "Baptism of the Holy Spirit,"* by Stephen B. Clark, especially p. 15.

Bibliography

Christenson, Larry. *Speaking in Tongues.* Minneapolis: Bethany Fellowship, 1968.

Clark, Stephen B. *Confirmation and the "Baptism of the Holy Spirit."* Plainfield, New Jersey: Logos International, 1971.

McDonnell, Kilian. *Catholic Pentecostalism: Problems in Evaluation.* Plainfield, New Jersey: Logos International, 1971.

Williams, J. Rodman. *The Era of the Spirit.* Plainfield, New Jersey: Logos International, 1971.

Faith and Order: Louvain, 1971. Geneva: World Council of Churches, 1971.

3

A New Era in History

A new era in history is now opening up before us in a fresh and powerful way. There is a working of the Spirit of God in our day that is bringing about a resurgence within Christendom of the vitality and dynamism of the early church. I refer to the Pentecostal or charismatic renewal which vividly represents the breaking in of this new era.

The Spirit of God doubtless is active in many ways making for the renewal of the church. One may rejoice at every evidence of the Spirit's work in such areas as worship, evangelism, Christian nurture, social involvement, and ecumenical activity. However, I know of nothing that more significantly shows forth a renewal in depth than the present charismatic movement. For herein is a concentration of the activity of the Holy Spirit that provides a personal and community dynamic which can bring about a radical transformation of all of life.

What we behold in this present movement of the Holy Spirit is, I believe, a recurrence of the primordial power of the New Testament church. Something is happening today that is more than just one possible renewal among many; it is rather a coming to expres-

29

sion of primitive vitality due not to natural forces but to the operation of the Holy Spirit. It thus has vast potential for the depth renewal of the church throughout the world.

Let us turn briefly to the New Testament period to note this primitive vitality and dynamism. The Christian community as "fellowship [*koinonia*] of the Holy Spirit" lived in the dimension of the Spirit's immediate operations. God the Father through the risen and exalted Christ had poured out His Spirit upon one person and community after another. As a result there was such an irruption of the Spirit as to produce extraordinary manifestations of spiritual utterance, mighty powers of witness and healing, manifold expressions of love and unity (e.g., see Acts 2, and thereafter). The Holy Spirit had penetrated all the levels of human existence, through the conscious and subconscious to the depths of the human spirit, bringing forth new powers. He had provided energy for the proclamation of the Gospel and the coming of new life to the bodies and souls of men. The Holy Spirit had broken into the usual ordering of family and society life and reconstituted it a rich unity in faith and love. It was the same Holy Spirit who multiplied His gifts within the Christian fellowship and gave constant direction to its daily activity.

What occurred in terms of "extra-rational" phenomena was striking demonstration of this primordial vitality and power. We do well to note two of these phenomena, tongues and prophecy. The first was doubtless the stranger of the two, and could be interpreted by outsiders as irrational nonsense (even drunkenness or madness). But for those of personal experience, utterance in tongues signified a deeply spiritual communication of praise, intercession, or even utterance of divine mysteries. This was, all in all, an immediate communication between man and God through the human spirit and Holy Spirit in intimate relationship. Man did the speaking, freely and joyously, but the Spirit gave the language. Thus there was the conjoining of the natural and the spiritual in a way beyond human comprehension. Prophecy likewise signified immediacy of address not, as with tongues, from man to God but from God to man. Here through the ordinary language of man, the "extra-rational" again occurred, for the words spoken in prophecy were not derived from human reflection but came by the direct inspiration of the Holy Spirit: He provided the message. This prophetic utterance not only made for edification of the community; it often had a penetrating effect on those who visited the community, laying bare the secrets of their hearts, and revealing God's presence. That prophecy was a sign of God's potent presence no one could doubt. In addition to tongues and prophecy there were other spiritual manifestations through which the early church expressed its life in the Spirit. Even where it was the matter of a "word of wisdom" or of "knowledge," or seemingly such ordinary appointments as "helpers" and "administrators," there was the same sense of its being an activity of the Holy Spirit, and, accordingly, not merely a rational or human capacity in operation.

The primitive Christian community was totally "charismatic," that is, operating by freely bestowed gifts — whether in terms of manifestations for the common good, the functioning of the body, or the maturation of the community in Christ. The all-important matter was the "gift" (or "*charisma*"), not natural human abilities. Anyone in the community, by virtue of the Spirit's disposition, might be "gifted" for the word of wisdom or of knowledge, for the performance of miracles or healings, for prophecy or discernment of spirits, for tongues or interpretation of tongues, for helping or administration (I Cor. 12). Regardless of background and learning anyone might be "gifted" to be an apostle, an evangelist, a pastor, a teacher (Eph. 4). To be sure, study and training consequent upon such a gift were important, but the primary matter was the gift. There were also gifts of enablement for serving, exhortation, liberality, and deeds of mercy (Rom. 12, I Pet. 4). In all of these the community functioned charismatically, the Risen Lord through the Spirit exercising His direct headship and rule through the gifts He bestowed upon men.

Further, there were no set forms or places of worship. Usually meetings were held in homes, and everyone was free to participate. Whomever the Spirit "anointed" could offer a song, a lesson, a testimony, even a revelation. This was to be done in orderly manner, but order was not the fundamental thing. There were no ordained "offices" (only ministries), no designated "sacraments," no codified laws or regulations, no official dogmas — just the assurance that Jesus was Lord by the witness and presence of the Holy Spirit. Nothing was fixed or rigid, for the whole community was living daily in the dimension of the Holy Spirit.

Much more could be said about this divine presence and compelling power in the New Testament community. God, to be sure, was still the transcendent Other, awesome and holy, but in Jesus Christ He had come in man's own flesh, and now through the Holy Spirit He again and again became the indwelling, empowering force of the Christian life. Here was transcendence/immanence in such fashion as had not been experienced before; and people went forth into the world God-inspired, God-filled, God-directed.

Their worship, their witness, and their work were under the dynamic operation of the Holy Spirit.

What, we may ask, is the record of the church following the New Testament period? One can only answer that almost immediately there was spiritual decline. For example, the letters of the post-apostolic Fathers bear little trace of the original spiritual vitality, and the free sway of the Spirit's rule and life is greatly diminished.[1] Charisma is soon understood to be conveyed by ordination, and sacraments become the established channels of the Spirit's activity. The church is increasingly viewed as an institution rather than a fellowship, and priestly and episcopal office deemed to be constitutive for the church's existence. Pneumatic ordering of the community gives way to legal administration, and the church comes to understand itself as controller and dispenser of the Spirit. The Spirit is thus domesticated and canalized, and little room is left for Him freely to anoint leaders, and to multiply His own gifts and graces.[2] For a time there are scattered references in early patristic writings to the gifts of the Holy Spirit, but it is not long before many of the gifts disappear. The situation is expressed thus by one fifth-century church Father: ". . . Without a doubt they [the miraculous gifts of the Spirit] accompanied the effusion of the Spirit in the apostolic age, but they have ceased long ago to

---

1. H. B. Swete writes in his *The Holy Spirit in the Ancient Church:* "When the student of early Christian literature passes from the New Testament to the post-canonical writers, he becomes aware of a loss of both literary and spiritual power" (p. 3).

2. Bultmann writes that "The Spirit is no longer the power that now and again breaks out in 'gifts' — the words and deeds and conduct of the believers — but is a power immanent in the institutions, particularly in the sacramental cult; it is the officebearers' equipment for office" (THEOLOGY OF THE NEW TESTAMENT, Vol. II, p. 114).

find a place among us."[3] Thus despite occasional out-breaks such as Montanism[4] in the second century, the picture is largely one of increasing officialism, institutionalism, sacerdotalism — and dimming spiritual vitality. The church lived no longer in the full dimension of the Spirit's spontaneous and enabling activity.

A word should be added about the doctrine of the Holy Spirit during these early centuries. References to the Holy Spirit in the ante-Nicene Fathers are relatively sparse (that is, in comparison with the New Testament), and seem to belong to a world of inadequate experience and understanding. This becomes, I believe, all the more apparent in early creedal formulations. The Nicene Creed of 325, after a lengthy affirmation about Christ — His being of "the same essence as the Father . . . Who for us men and our salvation came down . . .," says only, "And we believe in the Holy Spirit." Nothing is added about who or what He is or does.[5] Later at Constantinople (381) there is a lengthier and more significant statement about the Holy Spirit: "And [we believe] in the Holy Spirit, the Lord and life-giver, Who proceeds from the

---

3. Theodore of Mopsuestia. The quotation, from his commentary on I Thess. 5:19f., II Thess. 2:6, may be found in Swete, *op. cit.,* p. 262.

---

4. See, e.g., Maurice Bennett's *A Living Flame,* chap. 10, "Montanism: A Revival of Prophecy." Montanism represents the sad, and to be repeated, story of new impulses emerging in the church too powerful for established forms. Whatever the excesses and imbalances of such a movement, the pity is that the "living flame," which might have given light and warmth to the church, is simply put out.

---

5. One might of course say that one council cannot do everything, and since the urgent problem facing Nicea was Christological — growing out of the Arian controversy — that the brief statement concerning the Holy Spirit would not necessarily point to any failure in the church's life or understanding. However, I would argue that this very concern with the Christological question, and the concentration thereon, was occasioned partly by an insufficient pneumatology. If the church had worked out its Christology in more dynamic, even pneumatic fashion, there could have been both a more satisfactory understanding of the event of Jesus Christ and the significance of the activity of the Holy Spirit.

Father, Who is worshipped and is glorified together with the Father and the Son, Who spoke through the prophets. . . ." Quite importantly, some statement concerning who the Holy Spirit is, His procession from the Father, and His deity are affirmed — and this surely is progress beyond Nicea. However, His particular operation which stands at the heart of the New Testament witness is not at all mentioned. ". . . Who spoke through the prophets" is all that is said; but such would scarcely seem to move beyond an Old Testament understanding of the activity of the Holy Spirit.[6] The Western Church did later add the *"filioque"* clause (Toledo, 589 A.D.) — "the Lord and life-giver, Who proceeds from the Father *and the Son"* — in belated recognition that the relation of the Holy Spirit to Christ had been omitted. But even with this important addition of something integral to the New Testament witness, there is still nothing about the rationale of this procession: proceeded for what purpose, to whom, how, and so on. Even as late as this, there is no further word about the work of the Holy Spirit; just a repetition of "who spoke by the prophets." The church, therefore, while affirming the deity of the Holy Spirit, His place in the Trinity, hence His nature and person, and His relation to Christ, did not give sufficient consideration to the Spirit's operation in the life of man. Again, this suggests an inadequate experience and recognition of His activity which is so prevalent in the New Testament record and in the early Christian community.

---

6. George Hendry, in his *The Holy Spirit in Christian Theology,* writes regarding the Creed of Constantinople: "As a formulation of the Christian faith, the statement is patently defective, both by the standard of the New Testament and in comparison with the second article of the Creed in which it is incorporated . . . [there is] *absence of any reference to the distinctively New Testament work, of the Spirit"* (italics mine), pp. 37-38.

Thus there would seem to be a close connection between the diminution of the experience of the Holy Spirit and the church's rather limited creedal statements. The problem would surely lie with the former, for statements of belief basically reflect the life and experience of the community. The church lived no longer in the full dimension of the Spirit's presence and power, His gifts and graces, His spontaneity and freedom.

The Middle Ages represent no satisfactory improvement of the situation. There were many monastic treatises on spirituality, thus a concern for the inward life of prayer and the growth of the soul. Yet for the most part this concerned various practices designed to achieve a state of contemplation by the ascent of the soul through several stages. The Holy Spirit scarcely figures in this, except as the infusion of love; His coming to man to anoint and empower is little mentioned. It is more a matter of what man undergoes than of what the Holy Spirit does — and so the New Testament perspective is seriously neglected. Concern about charisms of the Spirit does emerge, but this refers not so much to I Corinthians 12 as to Isaiah 11.[7] Hence, the operation of the Holy Spirit known in the early Christian community does not clearly come into focus.

---

7. Thomas Aquinas does seek to deal with the charisms of I Cor. 12, in his section on "gratuitous graces" (*Summa Theologica*, II, II, Questions 171-178). Consideration is given, in order, to prophecy, rapture, tongues, word of wisdom and knowledge, miracles. However — to note two of these "graces" — prophecy is considered primarily as intellectual knowledge, though God-inspired ("the mind being enlightened to know an intelligible truth," 176), and tongues are viewed as the supernatural gift of foreign languages for the proclamation of the Gospel ("Paul and the other apostles were divinely instructed in the languages of all nations sufficiently for the requirements of the teaching of the faith," 176). Aquinas thus intellectualizes these "gratuitous graces," and fails to appreciate their spiritual dynamism. He also writes as if all of this were a matter of past history, and suggests no relevance of these gifts for the church in his day.

We may now turn to some consideration of the Reformation. Few today would deny the significance of the Reformation in the recovery of many important truths — such as the sole headship of Jesus Christ, the priority of Scripture over tradition, and justification by faith alone.[8] Also it ought to be stressed that the Reformers variously did speak of the role of the Holy Spirit in uniting men to Christ,[9] in inspiring Scriptures, in making faith possible, and in bringing about regeneration and sanctification. Surely all of these were great gains, but, I would urge, in the area of the Spirit's dynamic activity much was left unsaid.

Let us note three things. First, there was insufficient recognition of the extraordinary and unique event of the coming of the Holy Spirit. Despite all the discussion concerning the work of the Spirit in bringing men to Christ — hence the area of salvation — there was little said about the coming of the Spirit and the new situation this creates. It was not clearly understood by the Reformers that the Spirit not only points to Christ but also Christ to the Spirit, and that the coming of the Spirit is a decisive new event in the series of God's mighty acts. They did not see that beyond the actuality of salvation is the event of the Spirit's bestowal; indeed, they tended to view the latter as simply the applying of the former (thus Pentecost, the subjective side of Christ's work of redemption). Accordingly, by overlooking — even misunder-

---

8. H. Bornkamm in his book, *The Heart of Reformation Faith,* summarizes the "fundamental axioms" as "by faith alone," "by grace alone," "Christ alone," and "Scripture alone" (chap. 1).

---

9. Calvin, for example, begins the third book of his *Institutes of the Christian Religion* with a chapter on the Holy Spirit in which he states, against the background of what Christ has done for mankind's salvation (discussed in Book II), that salvation is without effect unless it becomes an internal reality. This can happen, Calvin adds, through "the secret energy of the Holy Spirit, by which we enjoy Christ and all his benefits."

standing — the event of the Spirit's coming, the Reformers failed to grasp the important New Testament dimension of the Spirit's activity wherein the people of faith are filled with God's reality and presence, fresh powers of praise and proclamation are brought forth, and their common life is led into new and dynamic expressions.[10]

Second — and following upon what has just been said — the Reformation was not able fully to break free from the structural rigidity of the medieval church. To be sure, much was done to crack open the monolithic structure of the Church of Rome and thereby to relieve a repressive condition. However, the churches of the Reformers did not succeed in recapturing the vision of a church guided by the Holy Spirit diversifying gifts and ministries as He wills. Their continuing stress on form and order was of course necessary, especially in light of the separation from Rome, and thus the importance given to such "offices"[11] as pastor and teacher. But the freedom in the Spirit to be led into new patterns was not fully realized. Further, the definition of the church as existing where the word is truly preached and the sacraments rightly administered[12] leaves much to be desired.[13] For

---

10. Thus the Reformers carry forward a failure in pneumatology which existed from the early church on. It had been recognized *(supra)* that the Spirit proceeded from the Father (and the Son — Western tradition), but the significance of this procession was not understood. Nor is it understood by the Reformers, despite their advances in talking about the Holy Spirit in relation to many areas of Christian experience. Theologically, since Constantinople the Holy Spirit has been viewed as equal with Father and Son, but in terms of the understanding of His own "proper" work there is a practical subordination.

---

11. Luther, for example, in his German version of the Bible, often translates the word *"diakonia"* (ministry) as *"Amt"* or "office." Thus there is a continuation of the idea of ecclesiastical office which began in the post-apostolic period.

12. E.g., Calvin in his *Institutes of the Christian Religion:* "Wherever we see the Word of God purely preached and heard, and the sacraments administered ac-

as important as preaching and sacraments are, it is only people living in the "koinonia" of the Holy Spirit who represent the true *ecclesia*. It is in such a fellowship of the Spirit (insufficiently recognized by the Reformation) that the charismatic ordering of the life of the community can again become a reality.

Third, the Reformers did not adequately grapple with the gifts (*charismata*) of the Holy Spirit. Calvin is a particular case in point. Many times in his writings he speaks quite appreciatively of such gifts as tongues, prophecy, and working of miracles, but he does not satisfactorily come to terms with them. This may be seen in that Calvin frequently speaks of these extraordinary workings of the Spirit not only as having ceased with the early church but also that this cessation was *quite proper*. One reason given for this is that God provided these gifts only for the early adornment of the Gospel: ". . . Those miraculous powers and manifest workings . . . have ceased; and they have rightly lasted only for a time. For it was fitting that the new preaching of the Gospel, and the new kingdom of Christ should be illumined and magnified by unheard of and extraordinary miracles."[14] Concerning the gift of tongues (to Cornelius and household) Calvin writes: ". . . So did they glorify God with many tongues. Also . . . the tongues were given them not only for necessity, seeing the Gospel was to be preached to strangers and to men of another language, but also to be an ornament and worship to the

cording to Christ's institution, there, it is not to be doubted, a church of God exists" (Book IV, chap. 1, sect. 9).

13. Emil Brunner astutely observes that "no one will suppose that one of the apostles would recognize again in this formula the Ecclesia of which he had living experience" (*The Misunderstanding of the Church*, p. 103).

14. *Institutes of the Christian Religion*, Book IV, chap. 19, sect. 6.

Gospel."[15] Another reason given by Calvin for the cessation of these extraordinary gifts is that man so quickly corrupted them that God simply took them away. He writes that "the gift of tongues, and other such things are ceased long ago in the Church"; and, Calvin adds, concerning the gift of tongues, that "many did translate that unto pomp and vainglory. . . . No marvel if God took away that shortly after which he had given, and did not suffer the same to be corrupted with longer abuse."[16] So whether because of no need for further extraordinary gifts or due to the corruption that soon came about, it is evident that for Calvin "miraculous workings" have long ago rightly ceased. Thus Calvin, like others before him, affirms the end of the miraculous gifts, but also goes farther: he assures the church that this cessation was altogether fitting, and implies that, since God Himself withdrew them, they are gone without possibility of return.

What all of this signifies regarding the Reformation is a blind spot concerning the primordial dynamism of the Holy Spirit. To the left of the classical Reformers were the "Enthusiasts" (or "spiritualists") who placed much emphasis on the area of spiritual vitality. They stressed, for example, the church as a shared fellowship of believers, cultivation of evangeli-

---

15. *Commentary* on Acts 10:46.

---

16. *Commentary* on Acts 10:44, 46. Since Calvin views the gift of tongues as having ceased, he may seem inconsistent in writing in his *Commentary* on I Cor. 14:5: "As it is certain that the Holy Spirit has here honoured the use of tongues with never-dying praise, we may very readily gather, what is the kind of spirit that actuates those reformers, who level as many approaches as they can against the pursuit of them." However, Calvin here, as reading of the context will show, is talking about the knowledge and value of foreign languages, and urges that we should pursue them. Still, there is a bit of inconsistency in that Calvin views tongues in the early church as a passing miracle — and therefore not to be sought — whereas here it is a knowledge to be cultivated and prized. In either event, it might be added, Calvin, like Thomas Aquinas, misses altogether the spiritual dimension of speaking in tongues.

cal fervor, and simplicity of organization and worship. They also tended to lay more weight on guidance by the Holy Spirit than direction of the Scriptures. The Reformers reacted strongly against the Enthusiasts, viewing them as "fanatics" who left Scriptures behind,[17] elevating their own guidance by the Spirit to the place of primacy. Still, these "Left Wing" people, however exaggerated some of their ideas and actions, were seeking a more radical New Testament renewal. They represented an attempt to make some further headway toward overcoming the formalism and institutionalism of the past.

There is not space here to follow in detail the way of the churches since the Reformation. One might mention, almost in passing, a number of events relating to spiritual renewal, such as the rise of Pietism on the continent, the incidence of Puritanism, Quakerism, and Wesleyanism in England, the "Great Awakenings" and the emergence of Holiness groups in America. Of these, I should like to touch upon a few that have particular bearing on the contemporary scene.

A word, first, about Quakerism, which arose in the seventeenth century. In its concern to move away from such things as institutional forms, ordained clergy, structured worship, and dogmatic formulas, there would seem to be a return to much of the New Testament pattern. Also at the heart of Quaker life is the emphasis on immediate religious experience (the "Light within") — without which Christianity is an empty faith. Further, there is stress on the power of Christ or the Spirit as that which is most needed by

---

17. Calvin warns against the "fanatics" who see no further need of Scripture because they claim to be taught immediately by the Spirit (note his *Institutes,* Book I, chap. 9, appropriately titled "Fanatics, Abandoning Scripture and Flying Over to Revelation, Cast Down All the Principles of Godliness").

the church. So writes George Fox, founder of the Quaker movement: "The Lord . . . said unto me that if but one man or woman were raised by His power to stand and live in the same Spirit that the prophets and apostles were in who gave forth the Scriptures, that man or woman should shake all the country. . . ."[18] Often in Fox's writing there is reference to people trembling before the word preached, and a number of instances are given of extraordinary healing and deliverance. Also Fox, and those after him, stress the importance in the gathered meeting for waiting on the Lord until His word can truly be heard and spoken.

One may see in this Quaker belief and practice a recapturing of many elements of the New Testament. However, two comments must be added about how fully this was accomplished. First, the "Light within," which is sometimes called by Quakers the Holy Spirit, tends to be viewed not so much as a light or power which becomes an actuality through the redemption in Christ but is understood as a resident fact of all men's lives. Thus this "Light" only needs to be recognized and elicited that men may come to truth and salvation.[19] But the New Testament pattern is quite otherwise: there is no "Light within" until Christ enlightens the inner darkness; and the Holy Spirit is He who is sent to those made new in Christ. Without the vigorous New Testament emphasis on the presence of the Holy Spirit as occurring only

18. *The Journal of George Fox*, p. 149.

19. So Fox writes: "I exhorted the people to come off from all these things ["outward temples . . . traditions and doctrines of men . . . hireling teachers" etc.], directing them to the Spirit and grace of God in themselves, and to the Light of Jesus in their own hearts; that they might come to know Christ, their free teacher, to bring them salvation, and to open the Scriptures to them" (*Journal*, p. 140).

through forgiveness of sins[20] and redemption in Christ, there is danger that "the power of the Spirit" (a frequent expression of Fox) may become indistinguishable from human assertion and activity, and the breaking down of ancient forms and practices little more than the work of the human spirit. Further a *man* or *woman* may "shake the country," but is this necessarily *God's* own shaking? Second, despite references made by such a commanding figure as Fox to extraordinary happenings — people frequently "quaking," and healings now and then occurring — there is no clear picture of the recovery of the primitive dimension of the Holy Spirit within the community. The Quaker meeting, while beautifully depicted as a time of silence, waiting, and speaking only by inward prompting, does not fully succeed in recapturing the New Testament picture of a community in which the Holy Spirit manifests His gifts and workings. There is more emphasis on inward silence than outward praise, and on simplicity and directness of speech than on charismatic utterance.[21]

Second, in regard to the Wesleyan movement of the eighteenth century one may note how it goes beyond the Reformation in a concern for entire sanctification or Christian perfection. As in Luther's teaching, there is emphasis on sin and justification, as

---

20. One searches in vain in Fox's *Journal* for any reference on his part to a personal conviction of sin, or of his own coming to salvation. He writes about himself, "When I came to eleven years of age I knew pureness and righteousness" (p. 66), and he never admits to a departure therefrom.

21. I have discovered no reference to tongues in Fox's *Journal.* Philip Schaff, in his *History of the Christian Church*, Vol. I, p. 237, however, speaks of glossolalia "among the early Quakers and Methodists." If Schaff is correct, I do not know when this appeared among the Quakers. It might be added that Roland Knox in his book, *Enthusiasm*, does not agree with this statement about either early Quakers or Methodists (see p. 551). I am inclined to agree with Knox, especially about the Methodists (whom I will discuss below). He may be right also about the Quakers.

in Calvin's there is stress on regeneration and sanctification, but in addition there is Wesley's conviction of the possibility of realizing perfection in this present life.[22] By the Holy Spirit we are daily conformed to Christ in the process of sanctification, but there may, and also ought to, come a time when the Christian is granted entire sanctification: a freedom from inbred sin, and the perfection of love. Wesley by no means minimizes the need for salvation of a deep, inward kind; indeed, without this there is no sanctifying Spirit at work within man. Wesley's fuller concern, however, is for the realization of that perfection which may occur in Christian life.

It is important to note, first, that Wesley's emphasis leads to a view of two great blessings, salvation and entire sanctification. Both are of faith, and though separated by years, each occurs instantaneously.[23] How does this sanctification come about? Wesley writes: "Expect it *by faith*; expect it *as you are*; expect *it now* . . . a poor sinner that still has nothing to pay, nothing to plead but 'Christ died.' " Again, in more activist fashion, he writes in answer to the question, "How are we to wait for this change?" the following: "Not in careless indifference or indolent inactivity, but in vigorous and universal obedience; in a zealous keeping of all his commandments; in watchfulness and painfulness; in denying ourselves and tak-

22. See especially Wesley's book, *A Plain Account of Christian Perfection.*

23. For Wesley's discussion of whether entire sanctification or perfection occurs gradually or instantaneously see *John Wesley* (ed. by Albert C. Outler), pp. 282 and 294. Instantaneousness is stressed in both accounts. In a letter Wesley puts this position succinctly: "A gradual work of grace constantly precedes the instantaneous work both of justification and of sanctification, but this work itself is undoubtedly instantaneous. As after a gradual conviction of sin you are justified in a moment, so after a gradually increasing conviction of inbred sin you will be sanctified in a moment" (Letter of June 21, 1784. I am indebted to F. D. Bruner's *A Theology of the Holy Spirit*, p. 38, for this quotation.)

ing up our cross daily; as well as in earnest prayer and fasting and a close attendance on all the ordinances of of God. And if a man dream of attaining it any other way, he deceiveth his own soul."[24] It is significant that Wesley does not lay stress on the Holy Spirit in the attainment of this perfection. He occasionally mentions that the Holy Spirit will bear inward witness when this comes about. It would therefore seem clear that, despite Wesley's "second blessing" teaching, there is no thought of a special coming of the Holy Spirit, and so, as with the Reformers, this dimension of the Spirit's work is still not recognized.

Wesley's attitude toward the New Testament *charismata* is likewise revealing. In his preaching there were many occasions of people being "deeply smitten," crying out in anguish, falling to the ground, even going into convulsions before they came to salvation. Wesley saw in this the convicting power of the Holy Spirit. But he never laid claim to "extraordinary operations" of the Holy Spirit; indeed he sought to defend his movement against them.[25] At one time Wesley preached a sermon in which, referring to "extraordinary gifts" such as healing, tongues, and interpretation, he says: "Whether these gifts of the Holy Ghost were designed to remain in the church throughout all ages, and whether or no they will be restored at the nearer approach of the 'restitution of all things' are questions which it is not needful to decide." And then shortly thereafter, he adds, "It was, therefore, for a more excellent purpose than this, that 'they were all

---

24. Quotations from *John Wesley*, pp. 282 and 294.

---

25. In separate letters Wesley wrote, "I deny that either I, or any in connection with me . . . do now, or ever did, lay claim to . . . extraordinary operations of the Spirit" (Nov. 4, 1758), and "I utterly disclaim the extraordinary gifts of the Holy Spirit" (Nov. 17, 1759). See *The Letters of the Rev. John Wesley,* ed. John Telford.

filled with the Holy Ghost.' It was, to give them . . . the mind that was in Christ . . . those holy fruits of the Spirit . . . love, joy, peace. . . ."[26] At least it can be said for Wesley that he goes beyond Calvin in envisioning the possibility of some future restoration of the extraordinary gifts; however, he does not view the matter as one of any great consequence.

Third, the stress on revivalism and holiness, especially on the American scene in the nineteenth century, began to bring about a new emphasis on the work of the Holy Spirit. The Holiness movement represents a continuation of Wesleyan theology in its stress on a "second blessing" of entire sanctification, or complete holiness. In this movement it became common to speak of this second experience as "baptism with the Holy Spirit," or "Spirit baptism."[27] Along with the Holiness movement was the growth of a revivalism that likewise came to speak of Spirit baptism as a second experience, but not one so much of holiness as of "enduement of power." Revivalists such as Finney, Moody, and Torrey came increasingly to

---

26. Sermon preached, August 24, 1744, on Acts 4:31 (*Sermons on Several Occasions,* Vol. I, p. 41). It is interesting to note that in another letter Wesley also said: "While we do not depend on supernatural activities of the Holy Spirit we do not believe miraculous activities of the Spirit have ceased. . . . I am not aware that God hath anywhere precluded himself from thus exerting His sovereign power, from working miracles, in any kind or degree, in any age, to the end of the world. I do not recollect any Scripture wherein we are taught that miracles were to be confined within the limits either of the apostolic or the Cyprianic age, or any period of time. . . ."

---

27. Though Methodist in its origins, the Holiness movement rapidly became interdenominational. Also there were a number of evangelicals variously related to the Holiness movement who were advocates of a "higher life." Among the Holiness and evangelical leaders were such men as W. E. Boardman, John S. Inskip, Robert Parsall Smith, F. B. Meyer, J. Wilbur Chapman, A. J. Gordon, Andrew Murray, and A. B. Simpson. A. J. Gordon in a chapter entitled "The Enduement of the Spirit" (in his *The Ministry of the Spirit* [1894]) writes: "For it is as sinners that we accept Christ for our justification, but it is as sons we accept the Spirit for our sanctification. . . . It is an additional and separate blessing . . ." (pp. 69-70).

say that the need of the church in its evangelistic efforts was power for witness. And this, "baptism with the Spirit" alone could provide.[28] It is this combination of revivalism and holiness that immediately prepared the way for the charismatic renewal of the twentieth century.[29]

Now in coming to the twentieth century we discover a fuller recovery of the primitive dynamism of the Holy Spirit in the rise of the Pentecostal movement. Pentecostalism (originating about 1901) represented a kind of merging of holiness and revivalism by adding to the second blessing of holiness a third blessing of the enduement of power. However, as in revivalism, baptism with the Holy Spirit was identified with the latter. Thus it was held that beyond conversion (or justification) and holiness (or sanctification) there was a further experience of empowering, which is baptism with the Spirit.[30] This empowering, furthermore, was understood not only for missionary activity (as

---

28. See e.g., Charles Finney's *Memoirs* where he describes his own "baptism with the Spirit" (pp. 17-18) and the need for this on the part of clergy in general (p. 55). Also see his *Power from on High,* chap. 4, "Enduement of Power from on High." R.A. Torrey's *The Baptism with the Holy Spirit* (1897) and his *Person and Work of the Holy Spirit* (1910) clearly set forth a second experience, beyond regeneration, of enduement of power. E.g., "In regeneration, there is the impartation of life by the Spirit's power, and the one who receives it is saved: in the baptism with the Holy Spirit, there is the impartation of power, and the one who receives it is fitted for service" (*Person and Work of the Holy Spirit,* p. 176).

---

29. Though there are charismatic aspects in both revivalism and holiness (some reference to tongues, for example, especially in the Holiness movement), neither emphasis represents the concern for charismatic life of the community that was to develop in the twentieth century.

---

30. Rev. Charles Parham, first leader of the Pentecostal movement (who had been, in turn, Congregationalist, Methodist, and Holiness) said a few days before his own Pentecostal experience: "Though I honor the Holy Ghost in anointing power both in conversion and in sanctification, yet I believe there is a greater revelation of his power" (*The Promise Fulfilled,* Kendrick, p. 50). It was the inbreaking of this power on January 1, 1901, that was the beginning of the modern Pentecostal movement.

with revivalism) but for the individual's and community's life of praise, witness, and edification. It was to be "filled with the Spirit" — with all that the fullness of God can mean. In this event of Spirit baptism — which many now began to experience — there was indeed the resurgence of the New Testament reality of the presence and power of God.

It is important to note the close connection Pentecostals recognized between baptism with the Holy Spirit and the charismatic manifestation of tongues, or glossolalia. We have noted how this phenomenon, along with many other extraordinary workings of the Spirit, became almost unknown after the first few centuries; how theologians such as Aquinas and Calvin were at a loss to understand its significance and viewed tongues only as an event of past history; how after the Reformation there is no experience of this kind by men such as Fox and Wesley. It should be added that there was some manifestation of tongues in the late seventeenth century among the Huguenots of the Cevennes ("the little prophets") and the Catholic Jansenists, and then in the early nineteenth century among the Irvingites of Scotland, but none of these occurrences was ever widespread. Nor did these movements stress the Pentecostal connection between a special event of Spirit baptism and glossolalia. It was in the linking of the two, and the emphasis on tongues as "initial evidence" of baptism in the Spirit, that Pentecostalism made its unique contribution.[31]

This article is not the place to evaluate the Pentecostal doctrine of tongues as "initial evidence," but to stress rather the point that the Pentecostals saw an

---

31. According to Donald Gee, Pentecostal leader, "It was the linking together of speaking with tongues and the baptism in the Holy Spirit that sparked off the Pentecostal revival" [*Pentecost,* No. 45 (Sept., 1958)]. See Bruner, *op. cit.,* p. 48, f.n. 34.

integral relationship between Spirit baptism — or being "filled with the Spirit" — and extra-rational utterance. To be "Spirit-filled" signifies that man in the entirety of his being, his conscious and his unconscious life, is now pervaded by the Holy Spirit.[32] The spirit as well as the mind is included; accordingly, the most primary form of utterance in this event is spiritual not rational. The tongue as the instrument of human utterance may speak in self-transcending fashion because the Holy Spirit is now freely moving through the human spirit. On the deepest level this utterance is extra-rational in the sense of not being in the ordinary language of the speaker; but very close to it is utterance in ordinary language which is also extra-rational in that it is not a result of the speaker's own rational reflection. The first is glossolalia, the second is prophecy — and in their occurrence witness is borne to the fresh opening up of the world of the Spirit.

Pentecostals by no means stopped with the extra-rational of tongues and prophecy. They also testified to experiencing the whole gamut of spiritual gifts such as healing, working of miracles, discernment of spirits, interpretation, word of wisdom, knowledge, teaching, and administration. It is significant that for

---

32. Karl Barth writes: "Where men may receive and possess the Holy Spirit, it is of course a human experience and a human act. . . . The whole man, right into the inmost regions of the so-called 'unconscious' is taken in claim" (*Dogmatics in Outline, p. 139*). Likewise Emil Brunner: ". . . the Holy Ghost seizes the heart, not merely the nous: it pierces the depths of the unconscious and even the very constituents of the personality" (*The Misunderstanding of the Church*, p. 48). I quote these words from Barth and Brunner not because they refer directly to such matters as tongues and prophecy but because what they say about the Holy Spirit claiming and piercing the unconscious makes "extra-rational" utterance plausible. Brunner adds that "we ought to face the New Testament with sufficient candour to admit that in this 'pneuma' which the Ecclesia was conscious of possessing, there lie forces of an extra-rational kind which are mostly lacking among us Christians today" (*ibid.* p. 48). We may be grateful that this lack is being remedied in the present charismatic renewal.

the first time since the early church the whole range of these spiritual manifestations was claimed, and people sought to order their personal and community life in terms of these New Testament operations of the Holy Spirit.

To summarize: Pentecostalism represented a crucial breakthrough in the realm of the Holy Spirit. The focus, as noted, was not the Spirit's work in salvation, or even in sanctification, but in the much-needed empowerment of Christian life. The Pentecostal movement came about not through a high-level conference of theologians, biblical experts, or an ecumenical council, but through ordinary Christians who were raising in a fresh way a long-neglected question — not about incarnation and atonement, not about sacraments, not about ministerial orders, and the like, but about the power they saw in the New Testament witness. They sensed that this power was missing or quite minimal in their own lives and experience. Thus the pressing question came to be: What is the secret of the recovery of that power? And what they essentially discovered was the New Testament "hot line," namely, the coming of the Spirit through Jesus Christ — to those who truly believed in Him — with such force as to penetrate and pervade their existence, to set loose hitherto unrecognized and unknown powers for praising God, for witnessing mightily with accompanying "signs and wonders," and for bringing about a pneumatic ordering of the whole life of the Christian community.

Now this Pentecostal reality which broke in at the turn of the twentieth century was generally too much for the various churches and religious groups to absorb. Even among many in the Wesleyan, revivalist, and Holiness movements — which had prepared the way for Pentecostalism — there was strong opposition. Vigorous exception was taken particularly to the joining of Spirit baptism and glossolalia. The older churches of Protestantism (such as Lutheran, Presbyterian, and Episcopalian) paid little attention, largely viewing the Pentecostal movement as emotionalism, irrationalism, sectarianism gone wild, and beyond the pale of serious consideration. With growing opposition on many sides Pentecostals soon found themselves being spurned, and, more and more, were forced into pursuing their own path. Most people of Pentecostal experience were quite ready to dissociate themselves from those who opposed this new movement, and sought in their own assemblies a larger freedom. Thus as the years went by, the Pentecostals became increasingly a kind of third force alongside Protestantism and Roman Catholicism.

Within a half-century the Pentecostal movement (which came to be divided into a number of denominations) had spread over a large part of the world, and in many places today is the fastest growing of all Christian bodies. Then about mid-century there came a new wave of Pentecostal experience among people here and there in historic Protestant churches. This occurred not so much among people of Wesleyan and revivalist tradition, but, surprisingly, among more formal churches such as Episcopal, Presbyterian, and Lutheran. What began in the fifties rapidly picked up momentum in the sixties until there was scarcely a Protestant denomination not feeling the Pentecostal impact from within. Then came an even greater surprise (than traditional Protestants becoming Pentecostally involved) when in the late sixties the same Pentecostal reality began to stir within the Roman Catholic Church. No one can fairly estimate the number of neo-Pentecostals,[33] or "charismatics," there are today, but it seems evident that the movement is really just getting under way. Far more significant than numbers, however, is the way in which mainline (or "classical") Pentecostals in many places are having fellowship, praying and working together, with their Protestant and Catholic brethren in a remarkable spirit of Christian unity.

What is quite different about the neo-Pentecostal, or charismatic, upsurge is the fact that it is going on *inside* the established churches and is helping to restore the dynamism of the early church. Though there have been a number of struggles within these churches, and now and then a minister or layman has been evicted because of his Pentecostal testimony, the traditional churches are beginning to open up. It would be too much to say that a groundswell of receptiveness and enthusiasm has developed, but a new climate is emerging. Many who were convinced that the "old wineskins" could not take the "new wine" of Pentecost (thus rejection or withdrawal being the only possibility) are finding that the church is not past renewal. The way has been prepared through the centuries by the church's continuing life and witness, and, rather than the Pentecostal reality being a foreign intrusion, many are becoming aware that what is happening today is indigenous to the church's own reality. For here is found a rejuvenation of ancient forms, and a fresh flowing of the Spirit to infiltrate every aspect of the church's life.

If it is true that the Pentecostal reality is helping to bring about a renewal within the historic churches, it is also the case that these churches have their own

---

33. By this term I refer to persons of Pentecostal experience in the historic churches. Often the term is reserved for Protestants, whereas Roman Catholics are called "Catholic Pentecostals."

contribution to make. Many have a long and meaningful confessional history, there is the experience of centuries of faith and worship, and numerous theological insights have been gained — all of this, and more, can bring depth and enrichment to the charismatic renewal. Pentecostalism, with its one great contribution to make in the area of the work of the Holy Spirit, needs the balance of other traditions. Furthermore, as a twentieth-century phenomenon, also largely American in origin, it has tended to take on a particular cultural conditioning and expression that is by no means essential to the truth of the Pentecostal testimony. Thus the historic churches have much to give in return for the making of a more complete witness to the Christian faith in our day.

To close: Truly an extraordinary spiritual renewal is beginning to occur across Christendom. We are seeing the release of the primitive dynamism of the early church in our own century. By no means is it happening without the contribution of our fathers in the faith who helped prepare the way. Still, there is something refreshingly new and challenging about a movement that has no denominational or confessional limits; for everywhere that people are caught up in the Pentecostal reality there is an air of discovery, of excitement, of joy. Furthermore, what an amazing sense of unity — among Protestants of all persuasions, "classical" Pentecostals, and Roman Catholics alike — is found in this renewal! Here is "spiritual ecumenism" of the richest possible kind — Christians everywhere sharing an abundant fellowship in the Spirit.

This is a new era in history. What is happening today, to be sure, is a resurgence of the power that broke out almost two thousand years ago, but it is now taking place *within* a Christendom long established and multiple in its forms. All over the world the way is thereby prepared, as it could not have been at the beginning of the Christian era, for this fresh outpouring of the Holy Spirit. At the first Pentecost, people were gathered together "from every nation under heaven" in *one place,* Jerusalem; but now Jerusalem is the world, with Christians in almost *every place.* As the Holy Spirit moves in mighty power over the earth, baptizing people from on high, we can but rejoice exceedingly! For this verily is the renewal of God's people: to carry forward their mission to the world with new strength and vision, and to live more fully to the praise of His great glory.

Bibliography

Aquinas, Thomas, *Summa Theologica,* Part II, II. London: Burns Oates & Washbourne, Ltd., 1922.

Barth, Karl. *Dogmatics in Outline.* London: SCM Press, 1958.

Bennett, Maurice. *A Living Flame.* London: Epworth Press, 1953.

Bornkamm, H. *The Heart of Reformation Faith.* New York: Harper and Row, 1965.

Bruner, Frederick Dale. *A Theology of the Holy Spirit: the Pentecostal Experience and the New Testament Witness.* Grand Rapids, Michigan: Eerdmans, 1970.

Brunner, Emil. *The Misunderstanding of the Church.* Philadelphia: Westminster Press, 1953.

Bultmann, Rudolf. *Theology of the New Testament,* Vol. II. New York: Chas. Scribner's Sons, 1955.

Calvin, John. *Institutes of the Christian Religion* (Library of Christian Classics: Vols. XX and XXI). Philadelphia: Westminster Press, 1960.

————. Calvin's *Commentaries: Acts. I Corinthians.* Grand Rapids, Michigan: Eerdmans, 1957.

Finney, Chas. G. *Memoirs.* New York: Revell, 1903.

———— *Power from on High.* Sussex: Victory Press, 1944.

Fox, George. *The Journal of George Fox.* New York: Capricorn

Books, 1963.

Gordon, A. J. *The Ministry of the Spirit.* Minneapolis: Bethany Fellowship, 1964.

Hendry, George. *The Holy Spirit in Christian Theology.* Philadelphia: Westminster Press, 1965.

Kendrick, Klaude. *The Promise Fulfilled.* Springfield, Missouri: Gospel Publishing House, 1961.

Knox, R. A. *Enthusiasm.* Oxford: Oxford University Press, 1950.

Outler, Albert C. *John Wesley.* New York: Oxford University Press, 1964.

Schaff, Philip A. *History of the Christian Church,* Vol. I. Grand Rapids, Michigan: Eerdmans, 1950.

Swete, H. B. *The Holy Spirit in the Ancient Church.* Grand Rapids, Michigan: Baker Book House, 1966.

Torrey, Reuben A. *The Baptism with the Holy Spirit.* New York: Revell, 1897.

――――. *The Person and Work of the Holy Spirit.* London: James Nisbet, 1910.

Wesley, John. *The Letters of the Rev. John Wesley.* London: Epworth, 1931.

――――. *Sermons on Several Occasions.* Vol. I. London: Wesleyan Conference Office, 1872.

――――. *A Plain Account of Christian Perfection.* London: Epworth, 1952.

4

Pentecostal Spirituality

These pages will be an attempt to sketch out some of the main lines of Pentecostal spirituality. The Secretariat for Promoting Christian Unity in Rome has suggested that the international Roman Catholic-Pentecostal charismatic dialogue ought "to relate realistically to Pentecostalism which appears as a movement, a spirituality rather than a systematic theology."[1] Since the first formal session[2] concerns "Scriptural Basis," it would seem important to delineate certain aspects of Pentecostal spirituality, noting here and there biblical evidences given. Hence this paper will be largely informational and will draw on a representative range of Pentecostal sources, thus allowing the Pentecostal witness to speak for itself. These sources, however, will not include Catholic Pentecostal writing (despite the rapid proliferation of such), but will be confined to classical and neo-Pentecostal (Protestant, Anglican) materials. Actually, as the Steering Committee paper on "Reasons for a Dia-

1. Part of a statement drafted in Rome (September, 1970) at the first informal meeting of the Secretariat with representatives of the Pentecostal/charismatic movement.

2. Meeting in Zurich, Switzerland, June 19-24, 1972.

logue on the World Level," says, "There is no essential difference between them in terms of the spirituality they all three embrace."[3] Thus what is written here will be in essence true of the worldwide Pentecostal movement, although there will be many extrinsic differences. It will be noted that, even with Catholic Pentecostalism not being discussed, there are some divergences between classical and neo-Pentecostal understanding.

The concern of this paper will be limited to basic Pentecostal spirituality, centering in the area of what is termed "baptism in the Holy Spirit," and will say little about the *charismata* of the Spirit. I might add that there are those who prefer to call this whole movement "charismatic" rather than "Pentecostal" perhaps for three reasons: (1) the name "Pentecostal" has become largely associated with a particular denomination or sect; (2) they are dissatisfied with much of the traditional Pentecostal viewpoint on "Spirit baptism"; (3) a conviction has grown that what is particularly important today is the renewal of the ancient *charismata*. However this may be, it would seem important, first of all, to understand Pentecostal spirituality as represented by most Pentecostals, and particularly the way in which "baptism in the Spirit" is viewed in itself and in various relationships.

I am listing at the end a brief bibliography of sources quoted in this paper. A much more comprehensive bibliography may be found in Frederick Dale Bruner's book, *A Theology of the Holy Spirit: the Pentecostal Experience and the New Testament Witness,* pp. 342-76.

---

3. After two informal meetings (September, 1970, and June, 1971), a Steering Committee of Roman Catholic and Pentecostal/charismatic representatives met

1. Pentecostals stress the *experience* of the Holy Spirit. The center of the Christian message is Jesus Christ, the Pentecostal will say, but what is critical for him is "the personal and direct awareness and experiencing of the indwelling of the Holy Spirit."[4] Thus Pentecostalism, while not pneumacentric as such, does make a strong witness at the point of personal, immediate, spiritual experience. Note: The concern is not experience as such, but the Holy Spirit who is said to be experienced, personally and directly. Thus the Christian life is a matter of the experienced presence and power of the Holy Spirit.

According to Professor James Dunn (non-Pentecostal New Testament scholar): "Against the mechanical sacramentalism of extreme Catholicism and the dead biblicist orthodoxy of extreme Protestantism they (the Pentecostals) have shifted the focus of attention to the *experience* of the Holy Spirit."[5] Bishop Lesslie Newbigin (non-Pentecostal churchman) has written that the Pentecostal answer to the question, "Where is the Church?" is neither in terms of a given message (where the pure word is preached and rightly understood) nor of a given structure (where there is continuation of apostolate) but "where the Holy Spirit is recognizably present with power."[6] Thus he calls for a recognition of the Pentecostals as representing "a third stream" which, along with Protestantism and Catholicism, is needed for the ecumenical church of our day.

Pentecostals tend to be quite wary of talking

---

in Rome, October, 1971, to plan for the first session in June, 1972. This quotation is taken from one of the papers drafted at the Steering Committee meeting.

4. Part of a statement drawn up at the first informal meeting in Rome.

5. *Baptism in the Holy Spirit*, p. 225.

6. *The Household of God*, p. 95.

about a "theology" or "doctrine" of the Holy Spirit. It is not that they are fundamentally anti-theological but that they fear the elevating of theology or doctrine to the first place. With the traditional definition of theology as "faith seeking understanding" the Pentecostals would largely agree; however, they would want to be sure that the faith was not merely formal or intellectual (surely not merely a *depositum fidei* to be accepted), and that it be profoundly experiential. Pentecostals are basically people who have had a certain experience; so they find little use for theology or doctrine that does not recognize and, even more, participate in it. They are convinced that the shape and content of their experience, which they believe to be of the Holy Spirit, is essential to the life and thought of the whole church.

2. Pentecostals focus on the coming of the Holy Spirit at Pentecost as *continuing event*. According to the systematic theologian of classical Pentecostalism, Ernest S. Williams, "To be Pentecostal is to identify oneself with the experience that came to Christ's followers on the day of Pentecost; that is, to be filled with the Holy Spirit in the same manner as those were filled with the Holy Spirit on that occasion."[7] Thus what happened at Pentecost (according to Acts 1 and 2, especially 2:1-4) is more than a once-for-all event; it is to be experienced today.

Pentecostals speak most often of this continuing event as "baptism in (or with) the Holy Spirit." Other terms, taken largely from Acts, include, from the divine side, the Spirit's "outpouring," "falling," or "coming upon"; from the human side, the person is said to be "filled with," or "receives," the Holy Spirit: thus "full reception." "Baptism in the Spirit," how-

---

7. *Pentecostal Evangel,* 49, p. 11. See Bruner, *op. cit.,* p. 57.

ever, is the term most often used because it expresses for the Pentecostal two things: (1) the *totality* of the event' viewing baptism as immersion, it signifies that the whole man is submerged in, activated by, the Holy Spirit; (2) the *uniqueness* of the event: like baptism in water, it represents a decisive, therefore unrepeatable, experience in Christian life.

The Pentecostal doctrine of the Holy Spirit is held in close connection with this event, or experience. F. D. Bruner writes:

> "The Pentecostal doctrine of the Holy Spirit (pneumatology) is centered in the crisis experience of the full reception of the Holy Spirit. . . . Pentecostal pneumatology emphasizes not so much the doctrine of the Holy Spirit as it does the doctrine . . . of the *baptism* in the Holy Spirit. For it is not so much the general biblical doctrine of the Spirit or, particularly, the Pauline doctrine of the walk in or fruit of the Spirit (Rom. 8; Gal.5), or the Johannine work of the Spirit Paraclete (John 14-16) from which Pentecostalism derives its name or its special doctrine of the Spirit, though it wishes of course to include all these emphases in its life. Pentecostal pneumatology is in fact primarily concerned with the critical experience, reception, or filling of the Spirit as described, especially, by Luke in Acts."[8]

The Pentecostal, going beyond Acts, also may use other terms to express this experience. Two particularly are "anointing" and "sealing." See, for example, classical Pentecostal Harold Horton's *The Baptism in the Holy Spirit,* pp. 11-13 — "The Baptism in the Spirit is an anointing," and "The Baptism in the spirit is being 'sealed' with the Spirit."

3. Pentecostals view the event of "Spirit baptism" as *distinct from and subsequent to conversion.* The coming of the Spirit, as such, has nothing to do with conversion. The Spirit to be sure is active in

---

8. *A Theology of the Holy Spirit,* p. 57.

61

bringing a person to faith and repentance (therefore conversion), but this is other than baptism in the Spirit. Spirit baptism may occur simultaneously with conversion, or happen at some time thereafter; but in neither case are the two identical. Don Basham (neo-Pentecostal) writes: "The baptism in the Holy Spirit is a second encounter with God (the first is conversion) in which the Christian begins to receive the supernatural power of the Holy Spirit into his life."[9] A second "encounter," a second "experience," a second "blessing"; such is typical Pentecostal terminology.

In early Pentecostalism there was often stress upon Spirit baptism as a third, distinct experience. The first work of God's grace is justification "by which we receive remission of sins;" the second work is sanctification "by which He makes us holy"; whereas "the Baptism with the Holy Ghost is a gift of power upon the sanctified life."[10](Here one sees connections with the Holiness movement of the late nineteenth century that laid stress on sanctification as a "second blessing" and often called it "baptism in the Holy Spirit.") Later classical Pentecostal teaching, however, has increasingly tended to minimize, or even disregard, a second work of sanctification as prerequisite to Spirit baptism;[11] neo-Pentecostals do not stress it at all. Thus, presently, Pentecostals by and large speak of Spirit baptism as a second experience of God's grace: not for sanctification of life but for empowerment to witness (see below). Sanctification (in its initiatory stage) is understood as being included in conversion,

---

9. *A Handbook on Holy Spirit Baptism*, p. 10.

10. Quotations from *The Apostolic Faith* of 1906, early in the Pentecostal movement. See Nils Bloch-Hoell (non-Pentecostal writer), *The Pentecostal Movement*, p. 45.

11. Again see Bloch-Hoell, pp. 125-30.

or is thought of as a lifelong process that may or may not include Spirit baptism.

An event of Spirit baptism as distinct from conversion is claimed to be the experience of many Pentecostals. Formerly, there was a crisis occasion of turning to Christ in faith — a true conversion; later there occurred the event of the Spirit in their lives. Scripture passages that are used to point to this are largely found in Acts: Acts 1 through 2:4 — the 120 who were already converts before the Spirit came; Acts 8:5-17 — the Samaritans who had believed, and were baptized, some time later received the Holy Spirit; Acts 9:1-19 — Saul of Tarsus, who had a crisis experience of the Risen Lord on the road to Damascus, three days thereafter was "filled with the Holy Spirit"; and Acts 19:1-7 — the Ephesian twelve who after hearing the word about faith in Jesus Christ and being baptized, received the Holy Spirit. John 7:39 is also frequently quoted — "Now this he said about the Spirit, which those who believed in him were to receive . . ." (hence a later reception of the Spirit by those who already believed), and Galatians, 4:6 — "Because you are sons, God has sent the Spirit of his Son into our hearts . . ." (thus a distinct experience from conversion by which one enters into sonship, and possibly occurring later).

Conversion is often used interchangeably with "regeneration," "new birth," even "salvation." Hence to be "born again" or to "be saved" is quite different from Spirit baptism. The belief in Christ whereby men come to salvation is not necessarily accompanied by the event of the Spirit. Thus the Assemblies of God officially say: "All believers are entitled to and should ardently expect and earnestly seek the promise of the Father, the Baptism of the Holy Ghost and fire. . . . This wonderful experience is distinct from and subsequent to the experience of the new birth. Acts 10:44-46; 11:14-16; 15:7-9."[12]

Pentecostals therefore go beyond other evangelicals, who likewise stress conversion-regeneration, by adding a subsequent experience of Spirit baptism. Many evangelicals identify regeneration with Spirit baptism and insist that every "born again" Christian has thereby received the Holy Spirit. To receive the Spirit, from this perspective, is part and parcel of becoming a new man in Christ. For Pentecostals, however, to become a Christian is one thing, to be a "Spirit baptized" Christian is another.

It should be added that there is at least one classical Pentecostal group that does not differentiate between conversion/regeneration and Spirit baptism. I refer to the Christlicher Gemeinschaftsverband Mülheim/Ruhr in Germany that dates back to the early twentieth century. Christian Krust, longtime leader, writes: "In the Christian Federation of Mulheim communities we understand by the term 'Spirit baptism' the same thing which other groups in Christendom call 'coming to a living faith,' 'conversion,' 'rebirth' or 'salvation from above.' "[13] Again, "The attempt to set forth Spirit baptism as in principle a separate, second spiritual experience different from rebirth has no scriptural basis."[14]Arnold Bittlinger, Lutheran neo-Pentecostal, independently holds the same position in writing: "We Christians do not look for a special act of receiving the Spirit in 'sealing' or 'Spirit-baptism,' but we know that the Holy Spirit dwells in each Christian and also in each Christian can, and wants to, become manifest."[15] Thus from this classical, and

---

12. Irwin Winehouse, *The Assemblies of God*, pp. 207-09.

13. See Walter J. Hollenweger, *Die Pfingstkirchen*, p. 181. My translation.

14. See Hollenweger, *Enthusiastiches Christentum*, p. 223. My translation.

neo-Pentecostal perspective — representing a small minority in the Pentecostal movement — there is no differentiation between being Christian and being Spirit-baptized.

4. Pentecostals understand the Holy Spirit as acting differently in conversion/regeneration and in the work of "Spirit baptizing." The Holy Spirit in the former experience brings about conviction of sin, contrition of heart, and unites the believer to Jesus Christ. As such, many Pentecostals say, the Holy Spirit dwells *with* the believer, acting in various ways upon his life. With the event of Spirit baptism another relationship occurs, namely, the Holy Spirit comes to abide *within*. Only thus is He the indwelling Spirit. Harold Horton spells this out in writing: "The Baptism in the Holy Spirit is the Spirit 'in you' as distinct from 'with you' — a very great distinction indeed (John 14:17). The Spirit is 'with' every believer as He was with the disciples before Pentecost. He is 'in' those who are baptized in the Spirit."[16] Derek Prince (neo-Pentecostal) follows the same pattern in saying that "without the influence of the Holy Spirit a person cannot be convicted of sin, cannot repent, cannot believe in Christ, cannot be born again. However, the fact that a person has received all these experiences is not by itself evidence that the Holy Spirit dwells in that person. . . . To receive the Holy Spirit as an indwelling personal presence is a separate and subsequent experience. It is the privilege—and the responsibility—of each believer to go on and seek this experience personally."[17]

Other Pentecostals, while agreeing on two experi-

---

15. *Der Frühchristliche Gottesdienst*, p. 9. My translation.

16. *The Baptism in the Holy Spirit*, pp. 13-14.

17. *From Jordan to Pentecost, p. 66.*

ences, hold that in the moment of conversion/ regeneration the Holy Spirit comes to dwell within, whereas in Spirit baptism there is an "infilling" or fullness of that same Spirit. So writes R. M. Riggs (classical Pentecostal): "They who are Christ's have the Spirit of Christ. The Holy Spirit baptizes them into the body of Christ, and the Holy Spirit resides in their hearts."[18] Before conversion the Spirit may have been with them, as with the disciples before the Resurrection, but when one believes in the crucified and Risen Lord the Spirit comes in. Here the text quoted is John 20:22 — "Receive the Holy Spirit" — which is understood as the Spirit of regeneration, the Spirit bringing new life. "The Spirit of God's Son, as the Spirit of conversion, came into their hearts on that occasion."[19] (Note the difference from Riggs who sees the Spirit's incoming only later at Pentecost.) But this indwelling of the Spirit which happens to all believers at conversion is only "the first step of the Spirit's incoming"; it needs the supplementation of the Spirit's coming not to indwell but to "infill," not to convert but to overflow. Thus there is both a Paschal and a Pentecostal gift and reception of the Spirit: but for different purposes. Dennis Bennett (neo-Pentecostal) also distinguishes between the Spirit's indwelling and a subsequent "infilling" or "outpouring": "To become a Christian is to have God come and *live in you . . . to be converted . . .* to be *forgiven . . .* to be *born again . . .*"[20] He calls this "the first step." The second step follows: "It is not salvation . . . but a second experience. . . . When we receive Jesus as Savior, the Holy Spirit comes in, but as

---

18. *The Spirit Himself* p. 44.

19. *Ibid.,* p. 44.

20. *The Holy Spirit and You,* pp. 11-12.

we continue to trust and believe Jesus, the Indwelling Spirit can *pour out* to inundate, or baptize our soul and body, and refresh the world around."[21] Bennett can also speak of the latter as the "receiving" of the Holy Spirit, wherein the indwelling Spirit is now "received" into the entirety of one's being.

According to the first pattern above (Horton, Prince), many, perhaps most, Christians know nothing of the indwelling of the Holy Spirit (how this can be related to Romans 8:9b — "Any one who does not have the Spirit of Christ does not belong to him" — is not clear). They may be "born of the Spirit" and yet not be tabernacles of the indwelling Spirit. Thus, passages in the New Testament about the Spirit within apply only to Christians who have had a "second experience." There is only one "coming" of the Spirit, the baptizing action of the Spirit for the believer, where He comes to dwell within. According to the second pattern (Riggs, Bennett), all Christians are indwelt by the Spirit (this is the result [Riggs] of the *Spirit's* baptizing us into Christ, but it is not the same as *Christ's* baptizing us in the Spirit, which is another action), but not all are baptized in the Spirit. Since the word "receive" is used in both John 20:22 for the "indwelling" and in Acts for the "infilling," there are actually two receptions of the Holy Spirit — one for regeneration, the other for fullness (How this can be related to certain passages in Acts is not clear, since there is little evidence of a double reception of the Spirit in such accounts as Acts 8, 10-11, and 19; even more difficult are such passages as John 7:39 and Galatians 4:6).

Because of the problems implicit in either position above, there is a growing tendency, particularly

---

21. *Ibid.*, pp. 18-19.

among some neo-Pentecostals, to speak of the "second experience" as a "release" of the Spirit. The terminology of "baptism" and "receiving" is not thereby given up, but (e.g., in line with John 7:38) the picture is more that of flowing out, a releasing therefore, of the inward Spirit. Bennett, for example, speaks of the power needed "to change the world" as coming thus: "By the acceptance of Jesus the Savior and by the release of the Holy Spirit in and through our lives — by a renewal of the experience of Pentecost!"[22] The book by Watchman Nee, entitled *The Release of the Spirit*, is read widely in Pentecostal circles, and carries forward this theme.

5. Pentecostals characterize the meaning of baptism in the Holy Spirit variously. Since it is understood to be an experience of God's presence and power breaking in or becoming manifest, the meaning is proportionate thereto.

Some Pentecostals speak of the experience as a *new sense of reality in faith.* Formerly God, Christ, had seemed distant or indistinct, but now through the Holy Spirit reality has dawned. "We know He is real" is a motto inscribed on one Pentecostal banner, and the testimony of many is that "for the first time *I know* the faith to be true." In similar vein Horton writes: "The baptism gives great assurance concerning all the experiences of our salvation: sonship, forgiveness, divine favour, hope of heaven. Whatever assurances we had before the baptism are intensified unspeakably. . . ."[23] The Christian life is said to take on new reality — a lively sense of God's presence, a rejoicing in Him, a freshness in prayer and worship.

Power, or empowering, doubtless is the main

22. *Nine O'Clock in the Morning,* p. 136.

23. *Op. cit.,* p. 12.

word used to express the character of the experience. It is evident that from the beginning of the Pentecostal movement the endowment of power is emphasized. Charles Parham, Methodist, then Holiness minister, and first of the Pentecostal leaders, shortly before his "baptismal" experience wrote: "I honor the Holy Ghost in anointing power both in conversion and in sanctification, yet I believe there is a greater revelation of His power."[24] The "greater revelation" came a few days later. Oral Roberts (formerly Pentecostal Holiness, now Methodist) describes this power as "enabling power," or "the power of enablement," first of all to be a witness for Jesus: "*to do* and *to be* with the force of an explosion."[25] This includes power to heal, to cast out demons, to do mighty works. Michael Harper's (neo-Pentecostal) book, *Power for the Body of Christ,* which deals with baptism in the Spirit, by title shows the same emphasis. The power, accordingly, is understood as an enablement of the individual and/or the community to carry forward witness to Jesus Christ. Pentecostals draw their chief biblical support for viewing Spirit baptism as power from Luke 24:49 — "And behold I send the promise of my Father upon you; but stay in the city until you are clothed with power from on high" and Acts 1:8 — "But you shall receive power when the Holy Spirit has come upon you; and you shall be my witnesses. . . ."

"Fullness of life" is another way of expressing the Pentecostal experience of Spirit baptism. This is understood to mean a Christian life with an interior sense of "joy unspeakable and full of glory" (I Pet. 1:8 KJV), of a deep feeling of inner peace, of the satisfaction of a profound hunger for God, and of a newfound

24. See Klaude Kendrick, *The Promise Fulfilled,* p. 50.

25. *The Baptism with the Holy Spirit,* pp. 6-8.

love for, and unity with, other people. Spirit baptism, in Pentecostal witness, often seems to specify more than what one has previously known and experienced; at other times it seems to suggest a new dimension of life one has entered upon. The word "fullness" expresses for the Pentecostal both the quantitative and qualitative difference in Christian life and both continuity and discontinuity in relation to what one has experienced before. Such Scripture as "I came that they may have life, and have it abundantly" (John 10:10), ". . . that you may be filled with all the fullness of God" (Eph. 3:19) is often used.

But to be "filled with (or by)" the Holy Spirit also means, for the Pentecostal, to be a *recipient of God's gifts.* To return to the theme of enablement (above), Spirit baptism is the investment of the individual and community with various gifts for edification of the body and service to the world. Hence there are exterior manifestations of the Spirit in terms, for example, of "word of wisdom," "word of knowledge," "working of miracles," "prophecy," "discernment of spirits" (cf. I Cor. 12), and the like. Thus the coming of the Spirit, so Riggs says, is "THE COMING OF DIVINE EQUIPMENT."[26] Spirit baptism is not "gifts" as such; it is the *gift* of the Spirit. However, the Spirit in being poured out is at the same time the investiture of the believing community with heavenly powers. Pentecostals often point out that the experience of being "filled with the Spirit" in Scripture is expressed in terms of prophecy, tongues, boldness of utterance, discernment of spirits, overflowing praise, and thanksgiving (e.g., Luke 1:15-17, 42, 67; Acts 2:4, 4:8,31; 13:9; Eph. 5:18-19). The Spirit is not without His gifts, or manifestations.

One classical Pentecostal (Horton) sums it up by

26. *Op. cit.,* p. 82.

saying that there is both an *expressional* and an *experiential* side of baptism in the Spirit. "On its expressional side the purpose of the baptism is power. But there is an experiential side as well." He continues (regarding the "experiential"):

"In the marvelous baptism the fainting human spirit drinks draught after draught of the satisfying Spirit of God. . . . Those blessed floods of satisfying water come rushing in in astonishing reality and startling intensity by the baptism in the Holy Ghost. The baptized believer is not only the empowered believer; he is the satisfied believer. 'They shall be abundantly satisfied, thou shalt make them drink of the river of thy pleasure.' "[27]

6. Pentecostals speak much of the background or preparation for the event of Spirit baptism. There is general agreement that the essential background for this experience is *conversion*, or *salvation*. So writes Riggs in a chapter, "The Baptism in the Holy Spirit, How to Receive It," in bold letters, "WE MUST FIRST BE SAVED."[28] Writes Basham, in italics, "*If you have not already done so, you must accept the Lord Jesus Christ as your personal savior.*"[29] He adds: "By no means should anyone who is not a believing Christian pray for baptism in the Holy Spirit." Thus faith in Jesus Christ that brings salvation is the essential background or preparation. Without this, Pentecostals urge, to seek for the Holy Spirit is meaningless, since it is only the believing Christian who can possibly receive. Further, without this saving faith, one may experience not the *Holy* Spirit, but some spirit of confusion and error.

A second preparation frequently mentioned for Spirit baptism is *heart purification*. Classical Pen-

27. *Op. cit.*, p. 24.

28. *Op. cit.*, p. 102.

29. *Op. cit.*, p. 100.

tecostalism with its roots in the Holiness movement often spoke (as we have noted) of sanctification as the second work of grace preparatory to baptism in the Spirit. Without separation from sin and cleansing of the heart, the Holy Spirit cannot be received. For example, one Pentecostal denomination in its declaration of faith says: "We believe in the sanctification which is subsequent to the new birth through faith in the blood of Christ . . . [and] in the baptism with the Spirit which is subsequent to the purification of heart."[30] Sometimes the word "obedience" is used in this connection, drawn particularly from Acts 5:32 ("the Holy Spirit whom God has given to those who obey him"). More recent Pentecostalism lays much less stress on the theme of heart purification (even as it tends to omit sanctification as a second work prior to Spirit baptism). One neo-Pentecostal writer urges that baptism in the Spirit is not "an attainment or reward based on some supposed degree of holiness."[31] However, another writer stresses that "we should repent of every known sin";[32] but he does not suggest sanctification as a prerequisite. Indeed, sanctification is more likely to be a result of baptism in the Spirit than the other way around.[33] Thus one discovers a movement increasingly away from the classical stress on a prior condition of sanctification. It is interesting, and perhaps significant, to note that it is the practice of some neo-Pentecostals to emphasize not so much cleansing of inward sin as the exorcism of evil forces. Bennett, for example, spends most of a chapter on "Preparing to Receive the Baptism in the Holy

---

30. The Church of God in Latin America; see Bruner, *op. cit.*, p. 97 f.n.

31. Don Basham, *Face Up with a Miracle*, p. 148.

32. Michael Harper, *Life in the Spirit*, p. 5.

33. Harper, *The Baptism of Fire*, p. 18.

Spirit,"[34] discussing contemporary occult practices, and suggests a prayer of renunciation for those who have been involved. Once these unholy spirits have been cast out, one may be filled with the Holy Spirit.

Prayer is usually stressed as preparation for receiving the Holy Spirit. On the one hand, this is understood as living a life of prayer in which the soul is prepared increasingly for God's fuller blessing. On the other hand, this is prayer that focuses particularly on the hoped-for gift of the Holy Spirit. The *Pentecostal Evangel* (largest circulating Pentecostal publication in North America) includes in each issue a creedal statement that mentions only prayer as a condition for receiving the Holy Spirit: "We believe that the Baptism of the Holy Spirit according to Acts 2:4 is given to believers who ask for it."[35] This does not mean, Pentecostals say, that we earn the Holy Spirit through prayer, for it remains a gift; but as we ask, and continue to ask, the way is prepared for God to pour out His blessing. "Insistence and persistence," says one writer,[36] are important. Here the Scriptures often adduced are Luke 11:5-13 and Acts 1:14, 8:15, 9:11, and 10:2.

Another aspect of preparation emphasized by many Pentecostals is *yielding.* Riggs writes in vivid manner:

> "Jesus is the minister who officiates at this baptism in the Holy Spirit. We present our whole being to Him. Body, soul and spirit must be yielded. . . . Thus yielded to our Christ, we are taken into His wonderful charge and submerged into the great Spiritual Element which is none other than the actual Person of the Holy Spirit. . . . There are many spiritual experiences which approximate the baptism in the Holy

34. *The Holy Spirit and You,* chap. 4.

35. See Bruner, *op. cit.,* p. 98 f.n.

36. Riggs, *op. cit.,* p. 104.

Spirit. . . . Utter and complete baptism in the Holy Spirit, however, is reached only where there is a perfect yielding of the entire being to Him. . . ."[37]

Some Pentecostals speak of this as "emptying," wherein the candidate for spiritual baptism lets go all barriers (perhaps of security, reputation, pride) and the Spirit freely moves into the void. Thus God may have His complete way.

Finally, Pentecostals often point out that *expectant faith* is important for Spiritual baptism. This is not simply the faith that looks to God for salvation, but the faith that holds firm to "the promise of the Father" that He will send the Holy Spirit. Some Pentecostals speak of this as a faith directed to the Holy Spirit, e.g., "As there is a faith toward Christ for salvation, so there is a faith toward the Spirit for power and consecration."[38] Many Pentecostals, however, do not speak thus of two directions of faith, for, they urge, it is the same Christ who saves who also baptizes in the Holy Spirit, and ultimately all comes from God the Father. The important matter is expectation, yearning, desiring the fullness of what God may impart, and believing that at the right time He will give it.

7. Pentecostals recognize no essential connection between *external rites and baptism in the Holy Spirit.* Here we shall consider water baptism and the laying on of hands.

First, it is to be noted that, in regard to water baptism, the most prevalent practice is that of immersion, and of "believers" only. Writes Bloch-Hoell: "On the whole, adult baptism is practiced all over the

37. *Ibid.*, p. 67.

38. Myer Pearlman, *Knowing the Doctrines of the Bible*, p. 316.

world by the present Pentecostal movement."[39] There are exceptions to this in a few classical Pentecostal bodies (e.g., the Methodist Pentecostal Church of Chile, the Christlicher Gemeinschaftsverband Mülheim/Ruhr in Germany, and the Pentecostal Holiness Church in America where it is optional), and among many neo-Pentecostals the practice of infant baptism continues. Water baptism is understood as having to do with conversion/regeneration but not in the sense of mediating or conveying such sacramentally; rather water baptism is primarily the believer's action whereby he expresses obedience to the commandment of the Lord. However, the all-important matter is the prior act of faith wherein occurs the new birth. Baptism is an outward symbol of this profession, but as symbol it has no integral relationship with the experience itself (whether performed earlier, as with infant baptism, or afterward in believer's baptism as a sign of the faith professed). Water baptism is by no means essential to salvation.

Thus since water baptism has to do with conversion, and only rather incidentally, it has no vital connection with Spirit baptism. One may read lengthy Pentecostal statements on "baptism in the Spirit" and find, if at all, only passing reference to baptism in water. Bruner has compiled, from six representative classical Pentecostal writers, lists of "conditions" for receiving baptism in the Spirit, and on only two of the six lists is water baptism so much as mentioned.[40] Even for the two who mention baptism in water, a reading of their material will show that it is included more as an aspect of obedience than as a vehicle or

39. *Op. cit.*, p. 166.

40. *Op. cit.*, p. 92.

means of grace. Pentecostals often seek to justify this lack of emphasis on water baptism by pointing to the record in Acts: (1) the 120 are baptized in the Spirit at Pentecost (2:1-4), but no stress is laid on their (presumed) prior baptism in water; (2) upon Cornelius and his household the Spirit is poured out, but this is prior to their being baptized in water (10:44-48); (3) the Samaritans believe and are baptized, but it is days later that they receive the Holy Spirit (8:12-17). Since some are baptized in the Holy Spirit without any reference to water baptism, some prior thereto, and some thereafter, why should we be concerned, the Pentecostal asks, to work out some formal, or sacramental, relationship?

There are, however, Pentecostals today, especially neo-Pentecostals, who are seeking to work out a closer connection between Spirit baptism and water baptism. The two baptisms, they are saying, actually belong together. Michael Harper, looking back at the early church, writes: "This blessing [baptism in the Spirit] was regarded in the early church as the completion of Christian initiation, distinct from water baptism, yet linked to it, and experimentally distinct also from regeneration. Full Christian initiation was not deemed to have been completed until every convert had been both baptized in water by the Church, and also in the Spirit by the Head of the Church, Jesus Christ."[41] Ideally, they should occur in immediate connection, but in sacramental practice (where baptism is followed by later confirmation) and in experience there is frequently a long interval between.

What then about the relationship between laying on of hands and baptism in the Spirit? Again, Pentecostals see no necessary connection. In practice, the

---

41. *The Baptism of Fire*, p. 20.

laying on of hands for Spirit baptism occurs every-where among Pentecostals, but this practice is never elevated to a necessity; and there are innumerable testimonies that the experience often happens with-out hands being laid. Basham writes of this matter in his *Handbook*, under the chapter 33 heading, *"Does one have to receive the laying on of hands to be bap-tized in the Spirit?"* His answer points out that in the five Acts accounts where people receive the Holy Spirit, three depict laying on of hands (Acts 8:18, 9:17, 19:6), but the other two (Acts 2:4, 10:44) do not. Thus, says Basham, there is ample justification for this practice, but no way of regarding it as essential: ". . . The laying on of hands for the receiving of the Holy Spirit is scriptural, often helpful, but not always necessary."[42]

Pentecostals, moreover, do not view the imposi-tion of hands as limited to any one person or religious order. They point out that in two of the three cases mentioned, apostles do lay on hands (Acts 8:18 and 19:6), but in the other, it is simply the matter of a Christian brother (Ananias) who lays hands on Paul (Acts 9:17). Not is the laying on of hands viewed as a sacrament, which carries with it both the necessity of proper ecclesiastical order and the understanding of a particular rite as essential to the gift of the Holy Spirit.

A further word about confirmation: It is seldom mentioned in Pentecostal literature and witness, and if so is usually viewed rather negatively. For example, Robert Frost (neo-Pentecostal) says, almost in pass-ing, "No longer is baptism followed by the laying on of hands for the fullness of God's Spirit in power. The rite of confirmation most closely follows this form, but

---

42. *Op. cit.*, p. 97.

even here no one really expects to receive and to respond as did the disciples at Ephesus under Paul's ministry (Acts 19:1-7).''[43] Michael Harper speaks of confirmation as *"verabschieden"* or "goodbye" to the church: it is not the rite of fullness of the Spirit but of leave-taking. The confirmand usually disappears thereafter from participation in the life of the church. "Today the low level of expectation and the vague concept of what is supposed to take place [in confirmation] is in tragic contrast to the powerful experience of Pentecost and the transforming effect it had on succeeding generations of Christians, until formalism and unbelief robbed the Church of its birthright in the Holy Spirit."[44] It can be seen, from the writers just quoted, that a part of the problem is that no one expects much to happen. Question: Does this make confirmation a purely formal matter, or could a part of the problem be lack of discernment as to what may really be going on?

8. Pentecostals see a close relationship between *baptism in the Spirit and speaking in tongues.* Classical Pentecostalism holds firmly to the position that the *initial evidence* of Spirit baptism is speech in "other tongues." The Pentecostal Fellowship of North America, comprising fifteen major Pentecostal bodies, includes in its eight-point "Statement of Truth" the following (No. 5): "We believe that the full Gospel includes holiness of heart and life, healing for the body and the baptism in the Holy Spirit with the initial evidence of speaking in other tongues as the Spirit gives utterance."[45] Thus though there is not a simple identification between baptism in the Spirit and

---

43. *Aglow with the Spirit*, p. 20.

---

44. *Baptism of Fire*, p. 14.

---

45. See John T. Nichol, *Pentecostalism*, p. 4.

tongues, it is clear that the two are intimately related, since the first sign of Spirit baptism is this speech.

Pentecostals date their twentieth-century beginnings from January 1, 1901, with the experience of a Miss Agnes Ozman at the Bethel Bible College, Topeka, Kansas, when Rev. Charles F. Parham prayed for her:

> "It was as his hands were laid upon my head that the Holy Spirit fell upon me and I began to speak in tongues, glorifying God. . . . I had the added joy and glory my heart longed for and a depth of the presence of the Lord within me that I had never known before. It was as if rivers of water were proceeding from my innermost being."[46]

This "initial evidence" was speaking in tongues, although it was also accompanied by joy, glory, presence of God, and the like. Rev. John Osteen (neo-Pentecostal) describes his experience thus:

> ". . . With my hands lifted . . . and my heart reaching up for my God, there came the hot, molten lava of his love. It poured in like a stream from heaven and I was lifted up out of myself. I spoke in a language I could not understand for about two hours. . . ."[47]

One might say from this description that the initial inward evidence was the "lava" of God's love, but the outward was speaking in tongues.

Neo-Pentecostals, while likewise convinced of the importance of speaking in tongues, often prefer to use such an expression as "normal accompaniment" (rather than "initial evidence"), and say that speech in tongues may occur later. Basham (in his *Handbook*) answers the question, "Can I receive the baptism in the Holy Spirit without speaking in tongues?" by giving what he calls "a highly qualified yes," but

---

46. See Kendrick, *op. cit.*, pp. 52-53.

47. See *Baptists and the Baptism in the Holy Spirit*, "Pentecost is not a Denomination: It is an Experience" (Osteen's personal testimony).

then adds in bold letters, "SOMETHING IS MISS-ING IN YOUR SPIRITUAL LIFE IF YOU HAVE RECEIVED THE HOLY SPIRIT YET HAVE NOT SPOKEN IN TONGUES." For, Basham adds, "Those Spirit-filled Christians who have not yet spo-ken in tongues will receive a precious added assurance of God's presence and power when they do."[48] Nor-mally, tongues accompany Spirit baptism as evidence of the "overflow," but because of various reasons (such as ignorance, fear, prejudice) there may be a delay. Neo-Pentecostals, like their classical brethren, see a vital connection between Spirit baptism and tongues. Larry Christenson (neo-Pentecostal) agrees that there are those who receive baptism in the Spirit without tongues, but he calls this a "gap" in their Christian experience, and adds: "To consummate one's experience of the baptism with the Holy Spirit by speaking in tongues gives an objectivity . . . sign . . . to remind one in a special way that the Holy Spirit has taken up His dwelling in the body."[49]

Pentecostals find in the Acts narrative vindica-tion for their position. In the five incidents describing the reception of the Spirit, three accounts specifically state that those receiving the Spirit spoke in tongues: Acts 2:4 (the 120 at Pentecost); Acts 10:46 (the centu-rion and household); Acts 19:6 (the twelve disciples at Ephesus). The other two descriptions of the Spirit's being received, Acts 8:17 (Samaritans) and Acts 9:17 (Paul), make no direct reference to such. This may be implied, however, in the case of the Samaritans (Simon the magician "saw" something for which he was willing to pay, Acts 8:18-19), and Paul writes to the Corinthians that he does indeed speak in tongues

48. *Op. cit.*, pp. 62-63.

49. *Speaking in Tongues*, pp. 55-56.

— "I thank God I speak in tongues more than you all . . ." (I Cor. 14:18). Thus the case can be made for "initial evidence" in several instances (if not clearly in all), or as "normal accompaniment" (based on at least three out of five incidents).

Pentecostals generally admit that almost all their evidence for a close connection between baptism in the Spirit and speaking in tongues is drawn from Acts. The disputed text from Mark 16:17 is often also quoted: "And these signs will accompany those who believe: in my name they will cast out demons; they will speak in new tongues. . . ." Classical Pentecostals seldom question the dominical authority of this text (since it is contained in the King James Bible); neo-Pentecostals, while sometimes more hesitant in using the text, suggest that it points at least to a very early recognition in the Christian community of the close connection between believing and speaking in tongues. More of a problem for Pentecostals is Paul's discussion of tongues in I Corinthians 12-14 where he depicts tongues as *one* of nine gifts of the Holy Spirit, and thereafter raises the question (which implies a negative answer), "Do all speak with tongues?" (I Cor. 12:30). How can speaking with tongues be "initial evidence" or "normal accompaniment" of Spirit baptism if it is only one gift among many? Here the Pentecostal answer is twofold: (1) there is a difference between speaking in tongues as *sign* of the Spirit's reception (thus possible for everyone) and as a particular *gift* for body ministry (which not all possess); (2) even in I Corinthians 12-14 where the concern is body ministry, Paul can still say, "I want you all to speak in tongues" (I Cor. 14:5). Hence there must be some way in which this speech is possible for all.

Finally, Pentecostals maintain the close relationship between baptism in the Spirit and speaking in tongues by virtue of what they understand to be happening in this baptism. Since Spirit baptism is an "overflow" of the Spirit in praise of God, ordinary speech may very well be transcended by the language of the Spirit. So writes Robert Frost: "It is the ministry of the Holy Spirit to bring such release to our lives when by faith we allow Him to fill us to overflowing with praise to the One who has set us free. . . . No wonder the apostle Paul exclaims with great feeling, 'I thank my God I speak in tongues more than ye all!' "[50] It is also to be noted that speaking in tongues is not viewed as communication to men but to God. David du Plessis writes: "Paul considered all speaking in tongues as prayer and always addressed to God, never a 'message' to men."[51] Hence the old idea that tongues was a miraculous gift of foreign languages for proclamation of the Gospel, or that a proper interpretation would bring about its inner nature as communication to men, is discountenanced. Since what happens through baptism in the Spirit is primarily a new opening to God by the Holy Spirit moving in the spirits of men, speaking in tongues is essentially a vehicle of the upsurge of praise and thanksgiving to Almighty God.

---

50. *Op. cit.*, p. 28.

---

51. *The Spirit Bade Me Go*, pp. 82-83.

Bibliography

Basham, Don W. *Face Up with a Miracle*. Northridge, California: Voice Christian Publications, 1967.

————. *A Handbook on Holy Spirit Baptism*. Reading, Berkshire: Gateway Outreach, 1969.

Bennett, Dennis and Rita. *The Holy Spirit and You*. Plainfield, New Jersey: Logos International, 1971.

Bennett, Dennis. *Nine O'Clock in the Morning*. Plainfield, New

Jersey: Logos International, 1970.

Bittlinger, Arnold. *Der Früchristliche Gottesdienst.* Marburgan der Lahn: Oekumenischer Verlag Dr. R. F. Edel, 1966.

Bloch-Hoell, Nils. *The Pentecostal Movement.* London: Allen and Unwin, 1964.

Bruner, Frederick Dale. *A Theology of the Holy Spirit: the Pentecostal Experience and the New Testament Witness.* Grand Rapids, Michigan: Eerdmans, 1970.

Christenson, Larry. *Speaking in Tongues.* Minneapolis, Minnesota: Bethany Fellowship, Inc., 1968.

Dunn, James D. G. *Baptism in the Holy Spirit.* Great Britain: SCM Press, 1970.

du Plessis, David J. *The Spirit Bade Me Go.* Plainfield, New Jersey: Logos International, Rev. Ed. 1970.

Frost, Robert C. *Aglow with the Spirit.* Plainfield, New Jersey: Logos International, Rev. Ed. 1970.

Harper, Michael. *Power for the Body of Christ. Life in the Holy Spirit. The Baptism of Fire.* Plainfield, New Jersey: Logos International, 1971.

Hollenweger, Walter J. *Die Pfingstskirchen (Die Kirchen der Welt:* Band VII). Stuttgart: Evangelisches Verlagswerk, 1971.

————. *Enthusiastiches Christentum: Die Pfingstbewegung in Geschichte und Gegenwart.* Zurich: Zwingli Verlag, 1969.

Horton, Harold. *The Baptism in the Holy Spirit.* London: Assemblies of God Publishing House, n. d.

Kendrick, Klaude. *The Promise Fulfilled.* Springfield, Missouri: Gospel Publishing House, 1961.

Nee, Watchman. *The Release of the Spirit.* Cleveland, Indiana: Sure Foundation, 1965.

Newbigin, Lesslie. *The Household of God.* New York: Friendship Press, 1954.

Nichol, John Thomas. *Pentecostalism (The Pentecostals).* Plainfield, New Jersey: Logos International, 1971.

Osteen, John. *Baptists and the Baptism of the Holy Spirit.* Los Angeles: Full Gospel Business Men's Fellowship International, 1963.

Pearlman, Myer. *Knowing the Doctrines of the Bible.* Springfield, Missouri, 1937.

Prince, Derek. *From Jordan to Pentecost.* Witney, Oxon: Gateway Outreach Ltd., n. d.

Riggs, Ralph M. *The Spirit Himself.* Springfield, Missouri: Gospel Publishing House, 1949.

Roberts, Oral. *The Baptism with the Holy Spirit.* Tulsa, Oklahoma: Private Printing, 1964.

Williams, Ernest Swing. *Systematic Theology.* 3 vols. Springfield, Missouri: Gospel Publishing House, 1953.

Winehouse, Irwin. *The Assemblies of God: A Popular Survey.* New York: Vantage Press, 1959.

5

The Holy Spirit and Evangelism

Many churches have recently begun to take an enlarged interest in evangelism. This is being done with both a sense of urgency and chastened humility. The urgency arises partly from the nature of the Gospel itself—that it calls for reaching the unreached— and also from the desperate need of the world for the message of redemption. The chastened humility stems from our candid recognition that we have not been making much progress. Here and there good results may be pointed to, but the overall picture is one of little lasting success. Still we know that we cannot give up, and so in many places fresh efforts at evangelism are again under way.

In this situation I would urge the importance of doing some basic thinking about the Holy Spirit and evangelism. For here, I am convinced, is the fundamental area that needs careful reflection. This has been so since the church first began to bear witness to the Gospel. Let us turn to the New Testament record where the first proclamation goes forth and examine the connection between evangelism and the Holy Spirit.

It is apparent that the Holy Spirit and evangelistic witness are closely related. This close relationship is evident both on the basis of the words of Jesus, "You shall receive power when the Holy Spirit has come upon you, and you shall be my witnesses" (Acts 1:8), and the fact that after the Holy Spirit did come (according to Acts 2) the witness of the early church was effective. The connection is quite clear: only the coming of the Holy Spirit to those who were to be witnesses for Christ made the work of evangelism possible.

It would also seem to be obvious from the record that what the Holy Spirit supplied was power: "You shall receive power. . . ." This, the disciples were told, they had to have; they could not proclaim the message in their own strength — nor even with a heightening or deepening of their own capacities. They must receive power from "on high" (Luke 24:49) — transcendent, supernatural power to do the job. The necessity for this was undeniable, for the task of evangelistic witness was that of bringing people to genuine repentance and to a new life in Jesus Christ (Acts 2:38). Natural means were insufficient; only the power of God could break through human self-sufficiency and create a new beginning. So it was with the early church: it is hardly different today.

This brings me to the matter of my specific concern. Do we as a church today—as ministers, as laymen, as individuals—have that power? This question by no means tends to minimize many other important matters, such as the most adequate means of communicating the message, the connection between word and deed, evangelism and its relation to the total mission of the church, but it does seek to focus on what is essential. Do we have that power, or, to use the words of Acts 1, have we "received" it? Surely if we are lacking here, everything else—no matter how sincerely, vigorously, even relevantly done—is to no avail.

To return to earlier remarks about "chastened humility": I believe that we are coming to admit frankly that we are wanting in that power. What happened on the Day of Pentecost was that they were "filled with the Holy Spirit" (Acts 2:4), and thereby empowered. Here is where we as a church feel our serious need: we are not so filled, we are empty—and powerless.

Now I should like to do a brief re-examining of the record in Acts and raise three basic questions: first, *who* were they who received the Holy Spirit, *what* was required for this to occur, and *what* was it like when it happened? These, I believe, are important matters that point the way to a new power. If so, we need to grapple with them, and ask how the answers apply to us today.

In reply to the first question: those who received the Holy Spirit were true believers in Jesus Christ. According to Acts 1, it was the eleven apostles, later supplemented by over a hundred others, to whom the promise was given. The gathering was wholly of "brethren" (v. 16) in Christ. They all were waiting for the promise to be fulfilled. It is important to note that the gathered disciples had lived through the death and resurrection of Jesus. This meant death to their old selves and the rising of new persons. Peter may symbolically represent all, for in his bitter tears of contrition the old proud self was broken through and a new Peter of true repentance and faith was born. To *such* a Peter—and the others with him—now forgiven by God's grace, the Spirit was promised. The Spirit, the Holy Spirit, could thereupon be received.

It is striking to observe that Peter's sermon on the Day of Pentecost brought people to a deep conviction of sin: they were "cut to the heart" (Acts 2:37). They knew and admitted their terrible guilt of having put to death the Messiah—and out of that shattering experience they came to true faith in Jesus Christ. The word of Peter to them is sharply etched: "Repent, and be baptized every one of you in the name of Jesus Christ for the forgiveness of your sins: and you shall receive the gift of the Holy Spirit" (2:38). Here, again, to those who pass through a life-transforming repentance and faith, wherein the grace of God's forgiveness is realized, the Holy Spirit is promised. Only such truly changed—or converted—persons could possibly receive the promised Holy Spirit.

Hence, it is to be emphasized today that those who similarly believe are in a position to receive the Holy Spirit—and, empowered thereby, to do the work of evangelism. We dare not overlook or disregard this simple but essential fact. What happened to Peter and the others was a passing from death to life. They had come through an overwhelming conviction of sin (Peter weeping bitterly, the multitude "cut to the heart") to a life-renewing repentance and faith. Only this radical and revolutionary change could prepare the way for the presence and power of the Holy Spirit.

Surely it must be the same today. Only radically changed people—true believers—can be used by God to change others. True believers are simply not to be identified with church membership. "All that hear the Gospel, and live in the visible church, are not saved: but only those who are true members of the church invisible."[1] Salvation and church membership are not the same thing—nor, to be blunter, is ordination to the ministry, office in the church, or even teaching in a seminary (!)[2] any assurance of true faith.

---

1. Quotation from Westminster Larger Catechism, A. 61.

---

2. Karl Barth wittily but trenchantly suggests that the theologian, for all his

If we are to evangelize we must be evangelized; if we are to help others to pass from death to life we must have made the passage ourselves. There is no substitute for this: the conversion of the church must precede the conversion of the world.[3]

The primary thing therefore that we must do is to ask ourselves, *who are we* who are talking about evangelistic witness? Is it possible that some of our failures in this realm have been due to a far too facile assumption that we are believers—in the radical New Testament sense of the word—but actually are not? If such is the case, our evangelism must begin at home, for unless we have truly appropriated the divine forgiveness through repentance and faith, we cannot witness to others.

Our second question is: What was required for the Holy Spirit to come? Here we must be careful in our answer, for in one sense nothing was required: it was "the promise of the Father" which He would generously bring to fulfillment. It was to be at His time, not theirs; it was to be His gift, not their achievement. Accordingly, they could do nothing to cause it to happen. They could no more produce the outpouring of the Holy Spirit than they could bring about salvation.

But, on the other hand, much was required. They had to "wait"—and the waiting called for prayer, much prayer. So, we read further, "they devoted themselves to prayer" (Acts 1:14). This was not to cause the Holy Spirit to come, for such were impossible, but for them to be prepared for the moment

"high-flown contemplation, explication, meditation, and application," might even be "unenlightened, unconverted, and uncontrollably corrupted." *Evangelical Theology,* pp. 83-94.

---

3. Bonhoeffer writes of the need for "the Church's conversion and purgation." Thereafter, he adds, "men will be called to utter the word of God with such power as will change and renew the world." *Prisoner for God,* p. 140.

(known only to God) when they would be ready to receive.

Nothing is said in Acts about the nature of what they prayed. However, that it was persevering supplication day in and day out is unmistakable. Though the disciples did other things than pray,[4] their devotion was to prayer; it was the center of their existence together. Moreover, it was not just prayer in general; it was rather for one very specific matter: the coming of the Holy Spirit. This they knew full well they had to have, for without the power of the Spirit they would never be able to witness for Jesus Christ. So it was expectant, faithful, even needful prayer.

What the disciples did in waiting before Pentecost may have been pointed to by Jesus in these words:

> "Ask, and it will be given you; seek, and you will find; knock, and it will be opened to you. For every one who asks receives, and he who seeks finds, and to him who knocks it will be opened. . . . If you then, who are evil, know how to give good gifts to your children, how much more will the heavenly Father give the Holy Spirit to those who ask him?" (Luke 11:9-10, 13)

The need for persisting in prayer, continuous asking for the Holy Spirit, is vividly emphasized. Ask, and keep on asking, seek, and keep on seeking, knock, and keep on knocking[5]—as those who believe this gift to be so important that they tirelessly pray for it. For God is one who delights to give what His children truly desire. Such is the way in which He gives His Holy Spirit.

I am quite convinced that none of this suits us too

---

4. The election of an apostle to succeed Judas occurred during their days of prayer (1:15-26). This would suggest that their devotion to prayer by no means excluded other activity.

---

5. This is the actual meaning of the Greek words used in this passage.

well: prayer over a protracted period of time like the disciples before Pentecost, or asking, seeking, knocking—God alone knows for how long. We're too busy for this, and it sounds so very impractical; anyhow would it *really* make any difference? Aren't we reminded in our secular, fast-moving age that "God is where the action is," not in a prayer closet? Shouldn't we be busy *doing* things for the kingdom, trusting the Holy Spirit is somehow already with us? No, none of this suits us very much. Maybe, however, there comes a day (could it be even now?) when we begin to suspect that much of our activity is pretty superficial, and that as a people we stand in serious need. It is then we may be driven back to basic things, and pray as we have never prayed before, something like this: "Come, Holy Spirit. Fill us with Your power that we may witness effectively for Jesus Christ in this present age."

We come finally to our third question: What was it like when the Holy Spirit came? What happened at Pentecost—out of which the power to witness was born? To answer this question properly is not easy, but I do believe it has tremendous importance for the whole church. If we know, we may have further incentive to seek—or, God forbid, turn almost fearfully away.

My own church has put the question this way: "Can we expect something as elevating as the disciples' experience on the Day of Pentecost? Need our experience of the Holy Spirit be accompanied by exactly the same descriptive events: the sound of a mighty wind and tongues of flame?"[6] I should like to

---

6. Guide to "Call to Repentance and Expectancy," Study 6 (Presbyterian Church, U.S., 1965). Two other questions in the Guide relate to what has just been discussed: "Have we left our upper rooms prematurely? How long should we engage in prayer and expectation before moving out to witness?"

suggest that whether "as elevating as the disciples' experience" or not, we can expect something "elevating" indeed, and if not "exactly the same descriptive events" as mighty wind and tongues of flame, that *essentially* the same thing can happen now. It may carry us beyond what we are accustomed to, hence there may be some uncertainty. But if we are willing to venture, it can be an experience of great richness and meaning.

Let us look carefully at the account in Acts. Jesus had said that the Holy Spirit would "come upon" His disciples ("when the Holy Spirit has come upon you" Acts 1:8), and when this did happen at Pentecost it was an overwhelming event. The Holy Spirit, for whom they had been waiting and praying, suddenly, unexpectedly came and filled the place where they were gathered. It was as unmistakable as the rushing of a mighty wind. Yet they knew it was God—His Holy Spirit—surrounding them on every side, present in unlimited manner. They were, to change the figure, bathed in His presence: as by a refreshing stream from on high.[7] God was there—in amazing fullness!

But that was only a part of the experience, and as rich as it was, there was more to come. This same Holy Spirit who filled the house now rested upon each one of them in vivid fashion, like "a tongue of fire," and then, to climax it all, He moved within—and filled them too. God was present without and within. The wind without was now a wind within, racing through their total selves. What followed was as ex-

7. Jesus also spoke of the coming of the Holy Spirit as a "baptism" — "Before many days you shall be baptized with the Holy Spirit" (Acts 1:5). Peter describes the event, in his sermon at Pentecost, as an "outpouring" ("He [Jesus] has poured out this which you see and hear" [Acts 2:33]. The various terminology of "filling," "baptism," "outpouring," etc., all point to the totality of God's spiritual presence with the disciples. The word "refreshing" is found in Acts 3:19 — ". . . that times of refreshing may come from the presence of the Lord."

traordinary as all else: they "began to speak in other tongues as the Spirit gave them utterance" (Acts 2:4).

Now let us pause to catch our breath for a moment. Do we sense what it is all about—even if we are a bit staggered perhaps? To be sure, the coming of God's Spirit is ultimately indescribable, since it is God Himself moving in a new and powerful way into the human situation which has been made ready. "Wind" and "fire" are only earthly symbols of an altogether un-earthly happening, but what occurred is unmistakable. The Holy Spirit had come *upon and into* the waiting disciples—and taken complete possession. So full were they with the Spirit that when they first began to speak, it was the Spirit who gave the words. Their tongues were flooded by the reality of God. Some have called this "ecstatic" speech or language[8]—but, however named, any human expression is a feeble analogy (like "wind" and "fire") of the inexpressible. For when God comes in His Spirit, a whole constellation of the extraordinary is set up, and no description really suffices. The point would follow that only those who experience this same Pentecostal reality can understand: for all others it is mystification indeed.

So it was on the Day of Pentecost. The assembled audience, knowing nothing of the background or rea-

---

8. E.g., Paul Tillich writes of "the disciples' ecstatic speaking with tongues" at Pentecost (*Systematic Theology*, Vol. III, p. 151). It is interesting that the New English Bible translates Paul's words in I Corinthians about "speaking in tounges" as "using the language of ecstasy" (14:2 and elsewhere). Though the word "ecstasy" does point to an experience of joyous intensity — which doubtless was there — the term is misleading for two reasons: first, "ecstasy" is a highly emotional word and implies a kind of uncontrollable mystical frenzy; second, the word suggests a human mood of high elevation — a going "beyond oneself." The record in Acts points to neither: the disciples are fully in control of themselves (indeed, for the first time, from Pentecost on!), and it is not that they have been lifted *up* to a high pitch: it is rather than the Spirit has come *down* and permeated their lives.

son for what was happening, and arriving on the scene when the disciples had begun to speak in "other tongues," were utterly baffled. Many of them, however, heard in their own tongues the disciples "telling . . . the mighty works of God" (2:11). It was the praise of God, praise offered in multiple tongues by the Spirit through the disciples' speech; it was as if all the world[9] were glorifying God for His wondrous deeds. To be sure the multitude listening were amazed and astounded. Some with less spiritual perceptivity categorized the "other tongues" as so much drunken gibberish ("They are filled with new wine"). But there can be little question: the disciples were not filled with wine, but filled with the Spirit. And the language they spoke was not irrational nonsense, but language given by the Spirit to the praise and glory of God.

We come now to the result. Out of this experience of the fullness of God's presence which overflowed in spiritual praise, the disciples proclaimed the message about Jesus Christ. Peter immediately thereafter spoke in the common language of all assembled, but his speech was not the same as before Pentecost. It was now laden with power—spiritual power. It was not great oratory or "enticing words of man's wisdom,"[10] but it was in "tongues of fire" lighted by the Holy Spirit. The amazing conclusion: a great number —some three thousand—that very day came to salvation.

Now, having rehearsed the familiar story of Pentecost, I make bold to say that what happened there needs also essentially to happen to us if we are to do

---

9. In Luke's words, "Devout men from *every* nation under heaven . . . *each* one heard them speaking in his own language." Thus it was the universal praise of God represented in the disciples' utterance.

---

10. To borrow Paul's language in I Corinthians 2:4 (KJV).

an effective job of evangelism. Of course we are not to try to go back nineteen centuries and seek to re-live the situation in Jerusalem (such were an exercise in fantasy); I do believe, however, that it is becoming increasingly clear to us in the church that we desperately need an outpouring of God's Spirit as at Pentecost. We may talk much about repentance, expectancy, prayer: but what does it all signify?

I shall try to specify what I believe it means. Above all it is a recognition that we need to be visited by the reality of God in such fashion that we know His full presence. To replace our emptiness must come His fullness: to awaken our spirits we need His Holy Spirit. When this *really* happens, His Spirit creates in our spirit such praise and thanksgiving that the deepest and richest utterances are of His devising, not ours. Furthermore, emerging therefrom will be a heightened joy in the use of ordinary speech to glorify His name and the power to witness in such fashion that men and women will come to hear and believe.

If this statement seems to be a bit radical, this is intentionally the case. For we live in a day in which the world never more needed to hear the message of salvation, but at the same time seems to be less interested in, or open to, what the church has to say. We need undoubtedly to speak a more relevant language, to find points of contact wherever possible, to re-evaluate our patterns and procedures—on and on. *But,* our primary need is for *power:* the power of God's Holy Spirit which alone can lead men to a deep conviction of sin and to faith in Jesus Christ.

Here, then, briefly by way of summary: first, our churches—that means all of us, pastors, teachers, laymen alike—need a candid re-evaluation of *who* we are. Are we "true members," that is, have we truly known and appropriated God's work of redemption?

Have we existentially been led by God's Spirit into such conviction of sin that we have cried out for God's mercy in Jesus Christ? Have we received God's gracious forgiveness—or been satisfied just to talk about it, or maybe forget it altogether? *Without this salvation there can be no effective witness for Jesus Christ.*

Second, wherever and whenever people come to a life-transforming repentance and faith, they are then in a position to wait and pray for the power of God's Holy Spirit. Have we become so preoccupied with other matters (even preaching, teaching, and many, many other good things!), or so caught up in the activism of our day that we are not willing to pay the price of persistent asking, seeking, and knocking? *Without this prayerful waiting there can be no effective witness for Jesus Christ.*

Third, the conclusion of such expectant prayer, by God's grace, can be the extraordinary, amazing event of Pentecost in our own generation. Have we been somewhat confused about it in the past (all this business of "wind" and "fire"—and especially "tongues"!), and maybe a little fearful about what the Holy Spirit would do if He really took over in our lives? The marvel, however, is that when God's Spirit does lay hold of people, they are moved to a new level of praise and thanksgiving—and the power of Almighty God begins to flow through in all they do. *Without this power there can be no effective witness for Jesus Christ.*

The church of Jesus Christ, thus redeemed, expectant, and empowered, can once again proclaim the Gospel in such manner that Christ may be lifted up and the world today find new hope and new life.

Bibliography

Barth, Karl. *Evangelical Theology: An Introduction.* New York: Holt, Rinehart, and Winston, 1963

Bonhoeffer, Dietrich. *Prisoner for God: Letters and Papers from Prison.* New York: Macmillan, 1958.

Tillich, Paul. *Systematic Theology,* Vol. III. Chicago: University of Chicago Press, 1963.

Westminster Larger Catechism. See *The School of Faith: The Catechisms of the Reformed Church,* tr. and ed. by Thomas F. Torrance. London: James Clarke and Co. Ltd., 1959.

Minutes: Presbyterian Church in the United States, 1965. "Call to Repentance and Expectancy."

6

The Holy Trinity

In a letter to a friend, Thomas Jefferson wrote of the "incomprehensible jargon of the Trinitarian arithmetic that three are one, and one is three." He then urged the importance of Christianity getting back to the "pure and simple doctrines" Jesus taught. This sentiment doubtless finds echo among many people in the church today. Would we not be better off to travel with less theological baggage — and jargon — and streamline our faith? Is it not hard enough to believe in one God without adding this mystification about a Holy Trinity? We often sing about "God in three persons, blessed Trinity." Is this view of God as Trinity meaningful or helpful in our time?

One answer sometimes given is that the Holy Trinity is an essential dogma of Christianity and must be accepted whether we like it or not. This doctrine belongs to the church's "deposit of faith"; it is affirmed in great creeds such as the Nicene and Athanasian; it accordingly is a fundamental doctrine in the life of the church. Anyone therefore who does not accept this dogma could scarcely qualify to be called Christian. Furthermore, belief in this dogma is sometimes said to be essential to salvation. The Athanasian creed, just mentioned, begins, "Whosoever will be saved: before all things it is necessary that he hold the Catholic faith . . . and the Catholic faith is this: that we worship one God in Trinity and Trinity in Unity, neither confounding the Persons nor dividing the substance. . . ." Finally, after many further, still more technical, statements, the Creed continues, "He therefore who would be saved must think thus of the Trinity." We had better "think thus" and so believe . . . or else forfeit our salvation.

However, it is not very compelling today to say: the doctrine of the Trinity belongs to the Catholic, universal faith; the church teaches, so we believe. Maybe one should grit his teeth and say, "If I have to believe it, I suppose I will"; but there seem to be increasingly fewer people who find themselves able to do that. Further, it may not be quite clear why holding a particular doctrine — thinking in a certain way — can have so much effect on one's eternal destiny. Is it really that important? Can we not travel a little lighter and perhaps be better off?

Protestants have traditionally sought to go back behind creed and dogma to the Scriptures themselves. To be sure, dogma and creed are important as representing the church's considered judgment about matters of faith. But for those in the Protestant tradition, the prior matter has been: if the Bible says so, we are summoned to believe in all matters having to do with faith and life. If the Scriptures, which are the Word of God, teach a doctrine of the Holy Trinity, then it is ours to attend to with profound seriousness — no matter how we may feel or think about it.

Actually, however, there is no doctrine of the Trinity in the Bible. The word "Trinity" is nowhere to be found, nor the language "one God in Trinity and Trinity in Unity," and certainly nothing about needing to believe this for salvation. What we do have,

100

however, might be called the raw materials for such a doctrine; for the New Testament is laden with the names of Father, Son, and Holy Spirit, while vigorously affirming that God is one. And though there is no suggestion that we must believe this for eternal blessedness, there is the witness that to be truly Christian is to live in the reality of God as Triune.

Materials for a Trinitarian doctrine may be found in such words as Matthew 3:16-17, ". . . the Spirit of God descending like a dove, and alighting on him; and lo, a voice from heaven, saying, 'This is my beloved Son, with whom I am well pleased.' " The Holy Spirit, or Spirit of God, is mentioned, Jesus is addressed as the "beloved Son," and clearly the voice is "the heavenly Father." Though this is no doctrine yet of a Triune God, the materials are here — and elsewhere — that will later lead to detailed theological formulation. Or take for example the apostolic benediction of II Corinthians 13:14, "The grace of the Lord Jesus Christ and the love of God and the fellowship of the Holy Spirit be with you all." These, along with other words like "there is no God but one" (I Cor. 8:4), afford further grounds for development of Trinitarian doctrine.

But, more significant than the function of the Scriptures as material for doctrine (with their implicit Trinitarian theology) is the witness of Scripture that Christian life is that lived in the reality of God as Father, Son, and Holy Spirit. The Scriptures nowhere suggest that to believe in God as Trinity, or Triune — or to "think God" in such and such a manner (often leading to speculation and abstractness) — is really the important thing. The concern is that people be introduced into the reality of God as Father, Son, and Holy Spirit. It is primarily the matter of a life to be lived, not a teaching or doctrine to be held.

The one most obviously Trinitarian verse in the

New Testament, Matthew 28:19, "Go therefore and make disciples of all nations, baptizing them in the name of the Father and of the Son and of the Holy Spirit . . ." contains nothing about teaching people that God is Triune (teaching follows in the next verse — "teaching them to observe all that I have commanded you"). Rather what is commanded is the act of baptizing "in" (or, better still, "into") the name. . . . The purpose of that part of the Great Commission, "Go therefore . . . baptizing" is not to make learners out of people in regard to God, but to introduce them into life lived in the reality of God as Father, Son, and Holy Spirit. Unfortunately, we tend to think of this verse too much in terms simply of a baptismal formula. We fail to recognize that it refers to the most extraordinary of human possibilities, namely, baptism into the reality of Triune existence.

The earliest disciples of Jesus did not, by any means, start with a doctrine of Holy Trinity. There was not yet any dogma, no New Testament Scripture. The only thing that they had ever heard about God numerically was that He was one and not three. The Old Testament had vigorously affirmed, "Hear, O Israel, the Lord our God is one Lord." This was not just doctrine they had been taught, it was also deeply ingrained in their life and experience. The early disciples, as orthodox Jews, were radical monotheists; they abominated anything by way of idolatry or polytheism that would possibly dilute their faith. They were Unitarian — quite far from being Trinitarian. Yet, something amazing happened in their experience: a band of orthodox, monotheistic, even Unitarian Jews began to speak about the one God as Father, Son, and Holy Spirit. Before too long the early church was baptizing people into this Triune Name. Such an extraordinary change was not due to better or higher instruction. This could not have brought it about. Like their earlier faith in the one God, the conviction of His reality as Triune was burned into their life and experience.

This change occurred over a period of years, and it happened because of their association with Jesus of Nazareth. First, they came to know and experience God as Father. The teachings of Jesus had much to do with this, for He frequently spoke of God as "heavenly Father" and taught His disciples to pray "Our Father. . . ." In many sayings and parables Jesus depicted God's paternal care. But, more than this, the disciples came to experience God as Father through their sharing with Jesus His trust, assurance, and confidence in the Father's will. It was a baptism into life totally caught up in the reality of God as Father.

Also something else began to take place in the faith of the disciples. They gradually came to the astounding conviction that in the flesh of this Jesus of Nazareth they were being confronted with the reality of God Himself! As time went on they began to realize that, however human Jesus was (of that they had no doubt), there was something mysterious about Him, something that human categories could not contain. This Jesus did things only God could do — or had any right to do. He forgave sins, He healed the helplessly crippled, He stilled the waves of the sea, He cast out demons, He raised the dead. The disciples found themselves (the shock of this is hard for us to imagine), orthodox Jews, addressing Jesus as Lord, falling down before Him in worship, and, climactically, becoming convinced of His resurrection after He had been put to death. They came to know Him as Savior too, for they received His gracious forgiveness after a terrible night of betrayal and denial; and they found new life in His name. How could they doubt it? Here was God in one who called himself "the Son of man"; was He not verily also the Son of God? Thus did they come to know and experience — shall we say, were baptized into — the reality of God as Son.

That of course is not the whole story; a very important part remains to be told. Some weeks following Jesus' resurrection came the Day of Pentecost. After much prayer and waiting these same disciples were suddenly visited by an overwhelming sense of God's presence and power. They came to know, to experience — all through their life and community — the dynamic reality of God as Spirit. They were "filled with the Holy Spirit" (Acts 2:4), and in the fullness of that event they broke forth into tongues of inspiration, they witnessed mightily and effectively to Jesus Christ, they found healing going forth from them, on and on. . . . What was it all about? Jesus was no longer with them in the flesh, but this was undoubtedly the same power of God that they had recognized operating in His humanity; and indeed they knew that it was coming through Him. It was not the Father, not the Son, but the Spirit flowing from the Father through the Son — and they were pervaded wholly by it. They truly were baptized into the Holy Spirit . . . and life would never be the same.

For these disciples, clearly, a statement about God as Father, Son, and Holy Spirit was not dogma, nor was it an abstruse teaching they had to accept for salvation. It was rather the reality of God wrought into their lives. It was not creed yet, or theology (such as "one God in Trinity and Trinity in Unity"). It was that which precedes all significant theology: event, happening, experience. They had been reluctantly, almost unwillingly, led into the reality of God as Father, Son, and Holy Spirit. They had entered into Triune living.

Now it makes sense to note how the early church sought to bring people into the same reality. Jesus of Nazareth as Risen Lord and Savior they proclaimed,

One sent by God the Father, and through believing in Him the Holy Spirit could be received. In some instances baptism was into the name of Jesus only (as in Acts) and hands were often laid for the reception of the Holy Spirit. But the important thing was that people know and participate in the full reality of God as Father, Son, and Holy Spirit. So do we find, in a climactic way, the words of Matthew, "Go therefore . . . baptizing them into the name of the Father and of the Son and of the Holy Spirit. . . ."

Thus what is vital in talking about the Holy Trinity is that it is not simply a doctrine to be embraced but a reality to be lived. Every Christian knows something about this Triune life through his baptism in the name of the Father, Son, and Holy Spirit. However and whenever the water was applied, the essential matter is that it was done in — or into — the name of the Father, Son, and Holy Spirit. This meant initiation into Triune living; but it may have been only the introduction, especially if this occurred in infancy. The important thing is to grow up into baptism, to enter into life lived in the reality of God as Father, Son, and Holy Spirit. The Westminster Larger Catechism contains the interesting question, "How is our baptism to be improved by us?" to which the reply in part reads, "The needful, but much neglected duty of improving our baptism, is to be performed by us all our life long . . . by growing up to assurance of pardon of sin . . . by drawing strength from the death and resurrection of Christ, into whom we are baptized . . . and to walk in brotherly love, as being baptized by the same Spirit into one body." How far have we grown up to what our baptism signifies? Is there neglect here so that we may still think of the Holy Trinity as a distant doctrine rather than living reality to be experienced?

The question might be put this way: How far

along are we? We may, in addition to baptism, have confessed publicly (as at confirmation) the faith into which we were baptized — and this is surely good. But have we come to the place of existential commitment and openness to God the Father, Son, and Holy Spirit? It is unfortunately the case that many people are still practically and experientially Unitarians (here, incidentally, may lie the problem about the Holy Trinity seeming like "incomprehensible jargon"). God the Father in some sense they know; there is some recognition of His fatherly goodness and provision. They can pray the Lord's prayer, "Our Father," with a modicum of conviction, but that is about all. Of Jesus Christ as Savior and Lord, however, they know personally very little — and perhaps even less about the Holy Spirit.

Concerning the former, one may recall the story of John Wesley, baptized and confirmed in the Anglican church, but who not until much later came to realize that he did not actually know Jesus of Nazareth and His salvation. To the Moravian who pointedly asked him, "Do you know Jesus Christ?" Wesley could only reply, "I know that He is the Savior of the world." Whereupon Wesley was asked the question that shook him profoundly: "True, but do you know that he has saved *you*?" Wesley did not really know this — not until Aldersgate some time later. About this life-changing experience he wrote in his journal, "I felt my heart strangely warmed. I felt I did trust in Christ, Christ alone, for salvation; and an assurance was given me that he had taken away my sins, even mine. . . ." Wesley had "grown up" to assurance of pardon; his baptism into the name of Jesus Christ was now a vivid reality. Have we gotten that far?

However, baptism is not only into the name of the Father and Son; it is also into the Holy Spirit. Here it may be that baptism is most neglected, for whatever may be known about the Father and the Son, practically and experientially, many would confess to know little about the Holy Spirit. They may not be in such sad case as those early disciples who, upon hearing Paul's question, "Did you receive the Holy Spirit when you believed?" replied, "No, we have never even heard that there is a Holy Spirit" (Acts 19:2). For they doubtless have heard about the Holy Spirit and have been baptized also into His name. But — the urgent question — have they come to know this in terms of a sense of God's presence and power? This means life claimed by God through Jesus Christ in a total kind of way, the Spirit of the living God probing the depths of the conscious and the unconscious, releasing (as on the Day of Pentecost) new powers to praise God, to witness compellingly in His name, to do mighty works that only He can do. Do we know this?

Here it may be that we have struck upon the greatest problem in the church today: the lack of power. There is a spiritual vacuum, a feeling of emptiness, a sense of impotence. Where, many are asking, is the dynamic reality of God's presence? In an article appearing in *The Christian Century*[1] entitled, "The Power of Pentecost: We Need It Now More Than Ever," the author asks, "Why in every sector of Christianity today . . . [is] there so little evidence of spiritual power . . .?" "I am haunted," he continues, "by the memory of Pentecost and its power surging into the hearts of the disciples long, long ago. Where is that power today? Can it come among us again?" Then, finally, he adds, "It is time we took Pentecost seriously and eagerly received a new infusion of the Holy Spirit."

How does this register with us? Are we haunted likewise by that New Testament picture of "power

1. May 13, 1970.

107

surging" through the disciples long ago; do we wonder too if that power may come among us again; are we disturbed about the lack of spiritual vitality, joy, and enthusiastic witness? Is the Holy Spirit, the vast area of Christian living, yet unfulfilled? If so, there is no other way than expectant waiting upon the Lord in a prayerful attitude of "Come, Holy Spirit, come. Baptize us with power from on high." This means a yielding of ourselves, a submission, a childlike saying yes to God — and a willingness for Him to possess us completely. And then it may happen; the Spirit of God is poured forth.

In conclusion: The Holy Trinity has been discussed not primarily as a matter of church dogma, or even as a Scripture teaching to be accepted, but as the summons to a life of Triune existence — life lived in the reality of God as Father, Son, and Holy Spirit. God grant that we may enter fully into this divine heritage.

In the name of the Father and of the Son and of the Holy Spirit. Amen.

LOGOS INTERNATIONAL ANNOUNCES

ANOTHER BEST SELLER

BY MERLIN CAROTHERS
ANSWERS TO PRAISE

$1.95   175   PAGES
FULL SIZE
~~100,000~~ FIRST PRINTING   PAPER
150,000

ALSO NEW!   PRISON TO   **PRAISE**

POWER IN

Both Books Combined in DeLuxe Hard Cover Gift Edition

Leatherette Binding — $3.95 List Price

NEW

SPECIAL COMBINATION OFFER — FULL SIZE

PRISON TO PRAISE

POWER IN PRAISE

New   **ANSWERS TO PRAISE**

Pre-wrapped together $5.40 retail value to sell for $5.00

Full book-sellers discount on $5.00 price

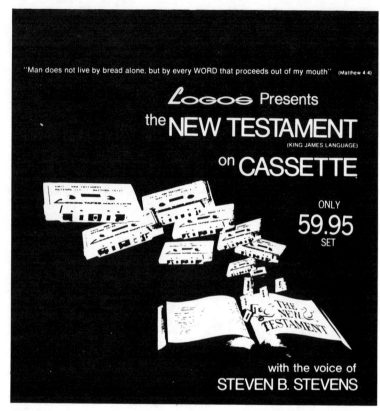

COMPLETE NEW TESTAMENT KING JAMES VERSION
  15 CASSETTES $59.95
CASSETTE TAPES BELOW ARE $3.95 EACH

JB1   JAMES BJORNSTADT, Author of "20th CENTURY PROPHECY"

SBC   RENEWAL IN SONG—Sampler Psalms

TA1   NICKY CRUZ, Author of "RUN BABY RUN"

TA2   (LTC) MERLIN CAROTHERS, Author of "PRISON TO PRAISE"

TA3   JAMIE BUCKINGHAM, co-author of "RUN BABY RUN"

TA4   ARTHUR KATZ, Author of "BEN ISRAEL"

TA5   DENNIS BENNETT, Author of "NINE O'CLOCK IN THE MORNING"

TA6   BOB BARTLETT, Author of "THE SOUL PATROL"

TA7   DR. RAY JARMAN, Author of "THE GRACE AND THE GLORY OF GOD"

TA8   MICHAEL HARPER, Author of "WALK IN THE SPIRIT"

TA9   BOB MUMFORD, Author of "15 STEPS OUT"

TA10 DR. HOBART FREEMAN, Author of "ANGELS OF LIGHT?"

TA11 DAVID duPLESSIS, Author of "THE SPIRIT BADE ME GO"

TA12 WENDELL WALLACE, Author of "BORN TO BURN"

TA13 DR. HOWARD ERVIN, Author of "THESE ARE NOT DRUNKEN"

TA14 CLINTON WHITE, Author of "FROM THE BELLY OF THE WHALE"

TA15 DR. ROBERT FROST, Author of "AGLOW WITH THE SPIRIT"

RECORDS

order from your local bookstore
or W.B.S.
Box 292
Watchung, N.J. 07061

SUGGESTED INEXPENSIVE PAPERBACK BOOKS
WHEREVER PAPERBACKS ARE SOLD
OR USE ORDER FORM.

A NEW SONG—Boone	AA3	$ .95
AGLOW WITH THE SPIRIT—Frost	L326	.95
AMAZING SAINTS—Saint	L409	2.50
AND FORBID NOT TO SPEAK—Ervin	L329	.95
AND SIGNS FOLLOWED—Price	P002	1.50
ANGELS OF LIGHT?—Freeman	A506	.95
ANSWERS TO PRAISE—Carothers	L670	1.95
ARMSTRONG ERROR—DeLoach	L317	.95
AS AT THE BEGINNING—Harper	L721	.95
BAPTISM IN THE SPIRIT—Schep	L343	1.50
BAPTISM IN THE SPIRIT—BIBLICAL —Cockburn	16F	.65
BAPTISM OF FIRE—Harper	8F	.60
BAPTIZED IN ONE SPIRIT—Baker	1F	.60
BEN ISRAEL—Katz	A309	.95
BLACK TRACKS—Miles	A298	.95
BORN TO BURN—Wallace	A508	.95
CHALLENGING COUNTERFEIT—Gasson	L102	.95
COMING ALIVE—Buckingham	A501	.95
CONFESSIONS OF A HERETIC—Hunt	L31X	2.50
COUNSELOR TO COUNSELOR—Campbell	L335	1.50
CRISIS AMERICA—Otis	AA1	.95
DAYSPRING—White	L334	1.95
DISCOVERY (Booklet)—Frost	F71	.50
ERA OF THE SPIRIT—Williams	L322	1.95
15 STEPS OUT—Mumford	L106	1.50
FROM THE BELLY OF THE WHALE—White	A318	.95
GATHERED FOR POWER--Pulkingham	AA4	2.50
GOD BREAKS IN—Congdon	L313	1.95

GOD IS FOR THE EMOTIONALLY ILL —Guldseth	A507	.95
GOD'S GUERRILLAS—Wilson	A152	.95
GOD'S JUNKIE--Arguinzoni	A509	.95
GOD'S LIVING ROOM—Walker	A123	.95
GONE IS SHADOWS' CHILD—Foy	L337	.95
GRACE AND THE GLORY OF GOD —Benson/Jarman	L104	1.50
HEALING ADVENTURE—White	L345	1.95
HEALING LIGHT—Sanford	L726	.95
HEAR MY CONFESSION—Orsini	L341	1.00
HEY GOD!—Foglio	P007	1.95
HOLY SPIRIT AND YOU—Bennett	L324	2.50
JESUS AND ISRAEL—Benson	A514	.95
JESUS PEOPLE ARE COMING—King	L340	1.95
JESUS PEOPLE—Pederson	AA2	.95
LAYMAN'S GUIDE TO HOLY SPIRIT—Rea	L387	2.50
LET THIS CHURCH DIE—Weaver	A520	.95
LIFE IN THE HOLY SPIRIT—Harper	5F	.50
LONELY NOW—Cruz	A510	.95
LORD OF THE VALLEYS—Bulle	L018	2.50
LOST SHEPHERD—Sanford	L328	.95
MADE ALIVE—Price	P001	1.50
MANIFEST VICTORY—Moseley	L724	2.50
MIRACLES THROUGH PRAYER—Harrell	A518	.95
NICKY CRUZ GIVES THE FACTS ON DRUGS —Cruz	B70	.50
NINE O'CLOCK IN THE MORNING—Bennett	P555	2.50
NONE CAN GUESS—Harper	L722	1.95
OUT OF THIS WORLD—Fisher	A517	.95
OVERFLOWING LIFE—Frost	L327	1.75
PATHWAY TO POWER—Davison	L00X	1.50
PENTECOSTALS—Nichol	LH711	2.50

PIONEERS OF REVIVAL—Clarke	L723	.95
POWER IN PRAISE—Carothers	L342	1.95
POWER FOR THE BODY—Harper	4F	.85
PREACHER WITH A BILLY CLUB—Asmuth	A209	.95
PRISON TO PRAISE—Carothers	A504	.95
PROPHECY A GIFT FOR THE BODY—Harper	2F	.65
PSEUDO CHRISTIANS—Jarman	A516	.95
REAL FAITH—Price	P000	1.50
RUN BABY RUN—Cruz	L101	.95
RUN BABY RUN—Cruz (Comic Book)		.20
SATAN SELLERS—Warnke	L794	2.50
SOUL PATROL—Bartlett	A500	.95
SPEAKING WITH GOD—Cantelon	L336	.95
SPIRIT BADE ME GO—DuPlessis	L325	.95
SPIRITUAL AND PHYSICAL HEALING —Price	P003	1.95
SPIRITUAL WARFARE—Harper	A505	.95
STRONGER THAN PRISON WALLS —Wurmbrand	A956	.95
TAKE ANOTHER LOOK—Mumford	L338	2.50
THERE'S MORE—Hall	L344	1.50
THESE ARE NOT DRUNKEN—Ervin	L105	2.50
THIS EARTH'S END—Benson	A513	.95
THIS WHICH YE SEE AND HEAR—Ervin	L728	1.95
TONGUES UNDER FIRE—Lillie	3F	.85
TURN YOUR BACK ON THE PROBLEM —Smith	L034	1.95
TWO WORLDS—Price	P004	1.95
UNDERGROUND SAINTS—Wurmbrand	U-1	.95
WALK IN THE SPIRIT—Harper	L319	.95
WE'VE BEEN ROBBED—Meloon	L339	1.50
YOU CAN KNOW GOD—Price	P005	.75
YOUR NEW LOOK—Buckingham	A503	.95

THE LOGOS INTERNATIONAL STUDY BIBLE

OLD AND NEW TESTAMENT: AMERICAN STANDARD VERSION
The world's finest Topical Analysis prepared by renowned scholars

WITH:--AMERICAN STANDARD TEXT (The Rock of Biblical
  Integrity)
  THE OLD AND NEW TESTAMENT
  VARIORUM RENDERINGS★   150 scholars offer special
                  helps, suggested word trans-
                  lations, meanings.
  TOPICAL ANALYSIS—A complete Bible analysis in one
                  volume.
  CROSS-REFERENCES—100,000 cross-references.
  INDEX, CONCORDANCE
  MAPS

IN ADDITION:--THE LOGOS LAYMAN'S COMMENTARY
          ON THE HOLY SPIRIT
          With special reference index on every verse in the
          New Testament referring to the Holy Spirit.

COMMENTARY EDITOR: **JOHN REA, Th.D.**—Biblical Research
                              Editor

CONTRIBUTING EDITORS: **HOWARD ERVIN, Th.D.**
                      RAY CORVIN, D.R.E., Ph.D.
                      ERWIN PRANGE, B.D.,Th.M.
                      DAVID du PLESSIS, D.D.
                      J. RODMAN WILLIAMS, Ph.D.
                      Fr. JOSEPH ORSINI, Ed.D.

Realizing the need for a quality but easily understandable HOLY
SPIRIT COMMENTARY, the editors combined their efforts in
supplying a verse-by-verse analysis of the New Testament.

★Variorum renderings are alternate suggested words and phrases taken from
ancient manuscripts and offered as alternatives by leading Bible scholars.
Ancient Bible texts, their meanings, origin, and scholars' opinions are included.

FREE
SAMPLE COPY
OF

Logos
An International Charismatic Journal

Worldwide Coverage
Feature Articles
Book Reviews
Trends

order blank on next page

------WHEREVER PAPERBACKS ARE SOLD OR USE THIS COUPON-------

WBS
Box 292, Plainfield, NJ 07061

SEND INSPIRATIONAL BOOKS LISTED BELOW

Title	Cat. No.	Price	
			☐ Send Complete Catalog
			☐ Free Sample copy of the LOGOS Journal

☐ 1 year subscription LOGOS Journal $3.00. Make payment to WBS, Box 292, Plainfield, NJ 07061

Name _____

Street _____

City _____ State ____ Zip ____